Sassy Feet!

Paint, Embellish and LOVE
Your Shoes (and Bags)!

MARGOT SILK FORREST

AND

DESTINY CARTER

For Erin, who continues to make my life
a dream come true, every single day, with her love,
courage, and fabulous sense of humor.
Thank you, too, for putting up with a landslide
of shoes - and handbags - in the house!
-Margot

For Lila Hudson, my grandmother, a woman
whose determination, spunk, irreverence,
sass, and uncanny ability to rock the boat
has kept her vivacious well into her nineties.
If you don't believe me, check out the video at
http://www.youtube.com/theboogiegramma
-Destiny

Acknowledgements

Our heartfelt thanks to Erin Perry, Jenny Bierbaum, Kathy Duguid, Suzanne Cholet, Annette Pierson,
Sandy Scrivano, all the amazing women and men at the Peninsula Wearable Art Guild,
and every student in every class we have taught across California and Nevada.
All of you have educated and inspired us!

ISBN-13: 978-1466260559
ISBN-10: 1466260556

www.sassyfeet.com
margot@sassyfeet.com
destiny@sassyfeet.com
glittersweatshop.typepad.com

Cover design & illustrations: Destiny Carter
Book design: Destiny Carter and Margot Silk Forrest
Cover and inside photos: Destiny Carter and Margot Silk Forrest
Photo manipulation: Destiny Carter
Author photos: Frances C. West and Destiny Carter

TABLE OF CONTENTS

Cinderella is proof that a pair of shoes can change your life.

ANONYMOUS

CHAPTER 1

WELCOME TO OUR WORLD

It has come to our attention that, despite all previous efforts by suffragettes, the women's liberation movement, and Twitter, there is still a distinct shortage of sassy women in the world. This is probably why there are so many black, brown and beige shoes in our closets. (Well, maybe not in *our* closets….) Once, Margot even witnessed a chic young woman trying on shoes at the chi-chi Manolo Blahnik store in London remarking ruefully, "I'd better take the black pair. They'll go with more things." We say, "To heck with that!"

Color makes people happy. Wear colors! Whether it's royal purple, lipstick red, lapis lazuli blue or the green of your dreams, wear it. And not just on your nails. Wear it on your feet! Take out those old shoes or go buy an inexpensive pair and experiment with lush, saturated colors.

Creativity also makes us happy. That's why time flies when we are doing something creative. We are totally focused on it. We are not worrying about the meeting the next day or the critical tone in our mother's voice last time we spoke on the phone. We are *absorbed* by our creative process, as if we were being literally absorbed into something greater than ourselves.

This is why women love crafts. The colors bring us joy and the creativity brings us connection with our deepest and largest selves. Besides, it's really fun to be able to say, "Oh, that? I made it myself!"

Which brings us back to sass. Way back when, women weren't supposed to show off or even take credit for their achievements. Again we say, "To heck with that!" What this world needs is more sassy women — women who aren't afraid to take risks, trust their own instincts, and express themselves! Being sassy is a GOOD thing — for us, for our families, and for the world. In fact, our dear old world needs us to be sassy, to have confidence, to say what we think and stop hiding our light under a bushel. Who knew you'd be saving the world by painting your shoes?

INDULGE YOUR WILD SIDE

Now, bearing in mind that we have given you Official Permission to express yourself, even go wild, we want you to dig around in the depths of your closet and pull out a pair of shoes you don't wear anymore. If not shoes, a handbag that never sees the light of day will do. We *all* have old handbags in our closets!

As you read this book, keep your shoes or bag nearby and see what ideas surface. We'll be showing you nearly 100 shoe and handbag designs, along with straightforward directions on how to do them. You'll discover that painting and embellishing your own shoes and handbags is surprisingly easy to do and seriously fun! Best of all, you'll end up with a closet full of non-black, non-brown, and non-beige shoes and handbags to accompany you on your equally colorful forays into the world. Maybe only the very rich can afford custom-designed shoes, but anyone with an interest can custom-design their own. That's why we call this "The Shoe-It-Yourself Movement."

SAME SHOE, DIFFERENT DESIGN

Transformation. At heart, that's what painting and embellishing shoes is about. Taking something old, unloved or unused and transforming it into something wild, witty and wonderful — or even just useful again. I've had some women in my classes simply paint a lime green shoe a nice quiet pewter, while others are busy painting their neutral-toned shoes copper, pearl blue or citrine!

The goal of this chapter is to open your eyes to the fact that you can make just a few changes to a shoe and completely transform the way it looks. Each example shows you the exact same shoe painted and embellished in different ways.

In fairy tales, shoes are often the vehicle of escape from humdrum lives.

RENOWNED PSYCHOLOGIST MARIE-LOUISE VON FRANZ

THE BLACK FLAT CHALLENGE

MARGOT: When I first thought about following my bliss and someday teaching women (and the occasional man) how to turn ordinary shoes into something spectacular, I set myself a challenge: I would take a perfectly plain, not too interesting black flat and see what I could do with it (even though I hadn't yet developed sophisticated skills in upcycling shoes).

I figured that if I could transform this plainest of shoes into something special—and do it again and again and again—I'd have no problem juicing up all manner of heels, sandals, boots, and sneakers.

The eight designs above use the simplest techniques of painting, stitching and gluing to create their effects. They are called (from left) Sweet Memories, Orchid Sunset (described on Page 38), Cherry Blossom, Midnight Rose, Celtic Pearl, Garden Party Ancient Spirals (Page 34), and Caribbean Seas. I take them with me to this day whenever I teach so my students can see what BIG results you can get from making easy changes to a very "vanilla" shoe!

SHADES OF TURQUOISE & GILDED GREEK GODDESS

MARGOT AND DESTINY: The seven curving and wrapping straps of this zip-in gladiator sandal enticed us to each take one shoe and see what we could do with it. The result is a fascinating study in how different a shoe can look, depending on what you decide to do with it.

Margot painted the seven straps in differing shades and tints of Limeira's (our favorite brand of leather/fabric paint) Pearlescent Turquoise. (For details see Shades of Turquoise, Page 12.) Destiny took a more dramatic route, painting her originally bronze sandal a matte black, then adding gold trim and an embellishment of three spirals topped by a yellow freshwater pearl. We often take along all the shoes in this section when we teach to give our students an eyeful of how differently identical shoes can look, once you add some sass!

GYPSY SUMMER & WORD PLAY

MARGOT: My shoe-painting journey began when I saw the pink sandals above on sale at a Bass Outlet for $12! I bought two pairs, one with a beige-gray sole, one with a black sole.

The shoe on the right comes from the first pair I ever painted. It uses 12 colors of Lumiere paint and a little stencil that looks like a vine. For details see Page 11.

The sandal on the left, Word Play, is poetry for the foot, made by stringing word beads (found in a scrapbooking store) onto narrow Ultrasuede tape, then gluing the tape down. Very different looks, both of which benefit from using a dramatic paint job on the insole.

BROCADE DREAMS & BLUE HAIKU

MARGOT: This shoe is a kitten heel with a fairly pointy toe. When I bought it to experiment with, I got a second pair at half the price, and I decided to see what I could do with similar treatments. I would use one solid color of Lumiere paint, put piping around the throat of the shoe, and add an embellishment on the outer side.

Brocade Dreams is painted Metallic Olive Green, then piped with floral upholstery piping. A band of the same piping is glued from the sole line up over the toe and down to the opposite sole line, making it look as if the shoe were constructed in two pieces. Rat tail and Mouse tail cord (narrow stain-covered cord) cover the pink edge of the piping, which would have shown on the outside of the shoe. A lovely brass stamping of leaves is stitched onto the side.

Blue Haiku is painted with Pearlescent Blue and piped with satin bias tape printed with an Asian motif. The edge of the piping is highlighted by a narrow line of black Ultrasuede tape, from which hang three little Asian charms. Little "tails" of the black tape extend below the charms. This shoe is so popular, we have created a kit for it, complete with paint, satin bias tape, Ultrasuede tape, charms, and detailed instructions. Just add shoes!

CHAIN OF COMMAND & IN THE SECRET GARDEN

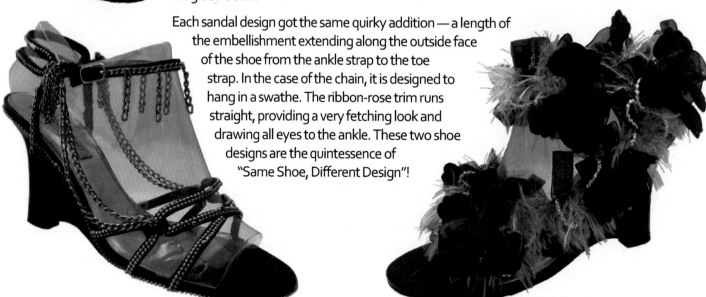

MARGOT: "Do you *wear* all these shoes?!" our fans ask us. No way! Both Destiny and I do wear shoes we've painted and embellished, but we also buy inexpensive and interesting-looking shoes to try out our design ideas and experiment on with new products. These little strappy sandals got entirely different treatments, once with colored curb and ball chain, the other with organza and chenille ribbon-rose trim. The chains were stitched into place, while the fabric trim (handily mounted on ½" elastic) was glued down.

Each sandal design got the same quirky addition — a length of the embellishment extending along the outside face of the shoe from the ankle strap to the toe strap. In the case of the chain, it is designed to hang in a swathe. The ribbon-rose trim runs straight, providing a very fetching look and drawing all eyes to the ankle. These two shoe designs are the quintessence of "Same Shoe, Different Design"!

High heels were invented by a woman who had been kissed on the forehead.

CHRISTOPHER MORLEY

A Few Things You Need To Know

Beyond encouraging the widespread outbreak of sass, our goal for this book is to show you the quickest and simplest ways to upcycle shoes and bags. The techniques and products we recommend are reliable and durable, so your great paint job or one-of-a-kind embellishment won't chip, crack, unravel, or fall off your fabulous shoes when you wear them.

And before we go any further, hear this: *You don't have to be able to paint in order to paint great shoes and bags.* In fact, you can create most of the projects in this book even if you can't draw a tree, paint a picture, bead a necklace, or sew anything more complicated than a single stitch.

Shoes To Try If You Think You Haven't Got A Crafty Bone In Your Body

To prove our point, here is a list of shoes in this book that can be created without any special talent for crafts or art.

- Several of the shoes in the Black Flat Challenge: Sweet Memories, Midnight Rose, Celtic Pearl, Garden Party and Caribbean Seas. Page 6.
- Shades of Turquoise: Seven straps, one luscious color tinted with white and shaded with black. Page 12
- Crocodile Mosaic: Like doing paint by number, but with designer results. Page 13.
- When in Oxford: One color of paint, a matching color of Glitter It glaze. Page 14.
- Fan Dance (at right): One color of paint, a simple cluster of embellishments stitched in place. Page 33.
- Raspberry Sherbet: Suede boots dyed a yummy color. Page 16.
- Little Violet: Toddler shoes painted pale violet, trim that's glued on. Page 47.
- Dancer's Delight: Organza flowers and silver leaf ribbon glued on. Page 47.

How To Use This Book

- **The Big Picture**

  First we'll show you how to paint (Chapter 2), then how to embellish (Chapter 3). Then we combine painting and embellishing to teach you some additional tricks and techniques. Later in the book, you'll see bridal shoes, handbags, and our *crème-de-la-crème* shoes.

- **How Chapters Are Organized**

  Each chapter opens with a gallery of shoes. You'll find before-and-after photos of shoe and handbag designs you can copy for your personal use. Or, let them serve as inspiration to create your own designs. Each design comes with a rating of the cost, level of difficulty, and patience needed.

  Within each chapter, projects are presented in order of simplicity, the easiest ones first.

  How-to information on doing the shoes or bags follows the gallery.

A Note on Terms and Brand Names

Here are some words you'll run into when you read this book, and here's what they mean.

- Lumiere — This is the brand of leather/fabric paint that we use most often when painting shoes and bags. It is an acrylic paint that water-soluble until it dries. After that, it is pure #&!% to get off, which is what you want in a leather paint! Lumiere is made by a company called Jacquard Products, and it comes in 25 colors. It is available in our online store.

- Neopaque Black — Also made by Jacquard, this is a similar leather/fabric paint that is a flat black. We use it to darken Lumiere. (Lumiere doesn't come in a black.) It is also in our online store.

- Angelus — This is the other brand of leather paint that we like to use. They also make good suede dye. Use Google to find sites that sell them online.

- Embellishment — This is the catch-all term we use to describe *all* the decorations you can attach to shoes and purses. It includes things like charms and baubles as well as fabric trims, fringe, feathers, old keys, you name it!

NOTE: If you use craft or artist's acrylic paints, or other paints not formulated for use on leather and manmade leather, you may get less-than-perfect results.

Why We Use Actual Brand Names for Products

We hate it when books tell you to use "glue" or "paint," but don't tell you what brands they think work best. That's why we name names. This is not because anyone is paying us to recommend their products. We should be so lucky....

The trade-off of our naming names is that you need to be understanding if the brands we recommend disappear from the market before we can update this book.

Anatomy of a Shoe: A Few Terms You Need to Know

The last thing before we get started is that it will help if you are familiar with the names for the parts of a shoe. That way, when I talk about gluing ribbon on the vamp, you won't wonder why she'd put up with such treatment. Other than the terms below, there's only one other word relating to shoes and feet that you'll need to know. It's "instep," and it refers to the top of your foot between the toes and your ankle. Your instep is the part of your foot that gets blisters the first time you wear clogs.

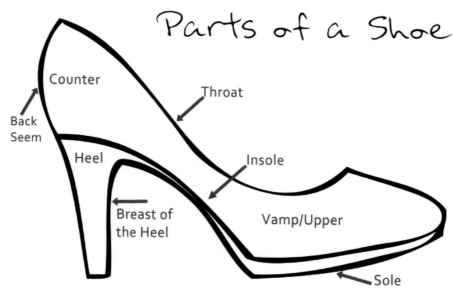

Parts of a Shoe

Give a girl the right shoes and she can conquer the world.

BETTE MIDLER

CHAPTER 2

PICK UP YOUR PAINTBRUSH!

Even if all you've ever done is paint by number, you can paint shoes! And if you're willing to experiment a little with colors, brushes of different shapes and our Glitter It glaze, you'll get results that will amaze you.

Here are the two best tips we can give you about painting shoes. First, don't be afraid of color. You have plenty of black, brown and neutral-tone shoes. How about some orange and violet ones? Or copper and rich blue? Remember, if you don't like the way they turn out, you can paint over them. Second, go further than you planned. The sandals below were only supposed to have different colored straps. When done, they looked boring. So we went further…

GALLERY: PAINTED SHOES

WHAT'S "LUMIERE"?

You'll hear this word a lot in this book. It's the brand name of our favorite leather paint. And no, we don't get money for recommending it! We just love the way it goes on and stays on, rain or shine. You'll find it by the bottle or kit in our online store. Since it doesn't come in black, we use a sister product called Neopaque.

GYPSY SUMMER

MARGOT: These were the first pair of shoes I ever did and to this day, I love them. I began by painting each strap in a different metallic shade of Lumiere paint. That looked sort of plain. So I pressed a stencil over each strap and sponged on some contrasting colors. Stenciling is an inexact science on leather, so I had to touch up the results with a small brush, but it worked!

Cost of materials: 🥿🥿🥿🥿
Level of difficulty: 🥿🥿🥿🥿
Patience required: 🥿🥿🥿🥿

PAINTING, PAGE 18
STENCILING, PAGE 20

Golden Zebra

MARGOT: I know, I know. These look really hard to do. They're not!

I started by painting the whole shoe with Limeira's Metallic Rust. Then I printed out a zebra pattern from the Web, and used a long thin brush to paint the black stripes. It didn't come out perfect, so I used the Metallic Rust to touch up the stripes. To my surprise, it looked really good. I left the back section of the shoe a solid brown for contrast.

Cost of materials: 👠👠👠
Level of difficulty: 👠👠
Patience required: 👠👠👠

PAINTING, PAGE 18

Shades of Turquoise

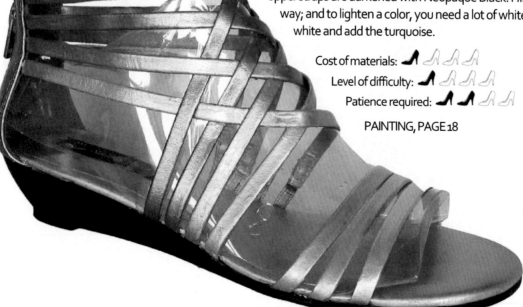

MARGOT: In one of the classes I taught, I watched a very talented silk painter adding larger and larger amounts of black paint to one of Lumiere's pearlescent colors. I was astonished at the beautiful colors that emerged. This seven-strap sandal uses progressive tints of Pearlescent Turquoise to create a range of shades. The untinted color is on the 4th strap. The toe straps are tinted with various amounts of Pearlescent White, while the upper straps are darkened with Neopaque Black. HINT: A little black goes a long way; and to lighten a color, you need a lot of white, so it's best to start with white and add the turquoise.

Cost of materials: 👠
Level of difficulty: 👠
Patience required: 👠👠

PAINTING, PAGE 18

CROCODILE MOSAIC

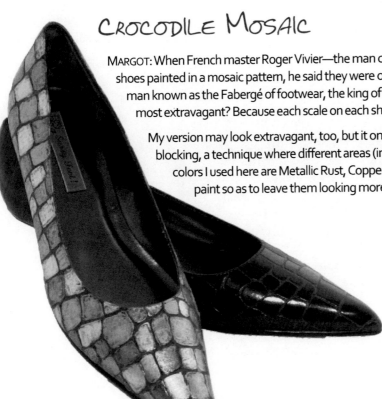

MARGOT: When French master Roger Vivier—the man credited with inventing the stiletto—created crocodile shoes painted in a mosaic pattern, he said they were one of his most extravagant designs. And this from the man known as the Fabergé of footwear, the king of the decorative shoe. So why were these shoes among his most extravagant? Because each scale on each shoe had to be painted by hand.

My version may look extravagant, too, but it only takes a single coat of paint. It's also a form of color blocking, a technique where different areas (in this case, of a shoe) are painted different solid colors. The colors I used here are Metallic Rust, Copper and Brass. I purposely chose to stroke on just one coat of paint so as to leave them looking more crocodile-like.

Cost of materials: 🥿🥿🥿🥿
Level of difficulty: 🥿🥿🥿🥿
Patience required: 🥿🥿🥿🥿

PAINTING, PAGE 18
COLOR BLOCKING, PAGE 20

RANGE ROVERS

MARGOT: It's impossible not to feel sassy when you're wearing a pair of cowboy boots. The angled heel, the shin-kickin' toe, the curved and stitched foxing on the vamp add up to an incomparably cool look. The problem is, really great cowboy boots can cost a small fortune. But if you're willing to put a little time and imagination into painting a pair, you'll have them at a fraction of the cost.

Thanks to the decorative stitching that divides a cowboy boot into neat sectors, it's like doing paint-by-number. The only difference is, the results are truly original. Before doing these, I browsed through some great photo books like *Cowboy Boots* and others by Tyler Beard and Jim Arndt to get ideas for color combinations. Then I chose my colors: Scarlet, Avocado Green, and Black (I used Angelus brand paints because I wanted flatter colors than Lumiere provides), and left part of the surface the original brown.

Cost of materials: 🥿🥿🥿🥿
Level of difficulty: 🥿🥿🥿🥿
Patience required: 🥿🥿🥿🥿

PAINTING, PAGE 18
COLOR BLOCKING, PAGE 20

Eyes may be the window to the soul, but shoes are the gateway to the psyche.

LINDA O'KEEFFE

ZOOT SHOES

MARGOT: The editor of a costume 'zine challenged me to create a pair of spectator shoes for an issue he was doing about styles from the 1930s. I hit the thrift store for slightly out of fashion white shoes, then started researching spectator shoe designs online. When I found one I liked, I printed out the design and went to work. I used drafting tape (one edge was cut with pinking shears) to block off the areas that needed to remain white. When the colored areas were painted in, I took a little silicone-tipped brush (called a Colour Shaper) and dabbed on the dots that simulated holes in the leather. From a distance, you can't tell they're not authentic!

P.S. Destiny says a toothpick works just as well as a Colour Shaper, — but I say, "Who asked her? I love my gadgets!"

Cost of materials:
Level of difficulty:
Patience required:

PAINTING, PAGE 18
FREESTYLE COLOR BLOCKING, PAGE 20

WHEN IN OXFORD...

MARGOT: After I'd been painting shoes for about a year, I suddenly thought, Is there some way to add glitter to shoes without it leaving sparkling but annoying bits all over the carpet? So I experimented with adding glitter to various leather paints and came up with Glitter It glaze, which you simply stroke on over your coat of paint.

Now, glitter might not be the first thing that leaps to mind when you think of oxford-style shoes, but I have a very mischievous streak that tempts me to put roses on Doc Martin's and heavy chain on delicate sandals. I painted these oxfords with Lumiere's Metallic Silver, then dabbed the saddle area with two coats of our Sparkling Silver Glitter It glaze. (It usually takes two coats to get the glitter glaze to cover evenly.) Then I changed the brown lace to black by sponging them with Neopaque Black, which is, of course, a fabric paint as well as a leather paint. The result? A sparkling and sassy update for a traditional shoe!

Cost of materials:
Level of difficulty:
Patience required:

PAINTING, PAGE 18
GLITTERING, PAGE 21

AUTUMN NIGHTS

MARGOT: Here's another traditional style shoe that's gotten a glittery update. This one combines the techniques of color blocking and glittering. Before applying Glitter It glaze, first paint the various areas of the shoe in background colors that are similar to the color of the glitter. I used Lumiere's Metallic Rust, Bright Gold, Super Copper, and Metallic Russet. Over those colors, I applied Sassy Feet's Glitter It glaze in Cognac, Antique Gold, Copper and Garnet. A sparkling and elegant update for a traditional shoe!

Cost of materials:
Level of difficulty:
Patience required:

PAINTING, PAGE 18
COLOR BLOCKING, PAGE 20
GLITTERING, PAGE 21

Before applying Glitter It glaze, paint the shoe surface in colors similar to the glitter you will be using. At right, Autumn Nights is shown after painting, but before the Glitter It glaze was applied.

DOODLESKIMMERS

MARGOT: I found these simple canvas skimmers on sale at Urban Outfitters and loved the way the side cutouts mimicked the peep toes. I painted the body of the shoe with Lumiere's Bright Gold, then brushed on Glitter It glaze in Antique Gold. As a finishing touch, I painted the white piping black around the throat of the shoe, on the peep toe and around the side cutouts.

At this point, I realized I hadn't gone far enough. All I had was a gold-glittered skimmer with black piping. It needed MORE! So I took a ¼" flat brush and painted "stripes" in Metallic Olive Green. The final touch was painting the insole black and cutting my own open-square stamp out of a dense eraser for dabbing on little squares of Metallic Olive Green squares.

Cost of materials:
Level of difficulty:
Patience required:

PAINTING, PAGE 18
PAINTING INSOLES, PAGE 20
STAMPING, PAGE 44

LADYBUG

MARGOT: As much fun as it is to paint shoes, painting little girls' shoes is even more fun! First of all, they're pretty adorable to start with. Second, they don't take a lot of work because they're so small. Third, you can do sweet, silly and sassy things and the little girl in your life will love it!

These Mary Janes were color-blocked by painting the lower ¾ of the shoe with Lumiere's Crimson. Next I brushed on Glitter It glaze in Really Red. The crowning touch was to dab on polka dots of Crimson using a silicone-tipped brush, called a Colour Shaper.

For another pair of tiny shoes, see Destiny's flower girl shoes, Delicata, on Page 46.

Cost of materials:
Level of difficulty:
Patience required:

PAINTING, PAGE 18
GLITTERING, PAGE 21

RASPERRY SHERBET

MARGOT: People often ask me if they can paint suede, and the answer is yes. But you lose the lovely soft feeling of suede when you do. As an alternative, I recommend dying suede using Angelus brand suede dye. These Uggs started out sand color — but I'm not a sand-color kind of girl. Purple? Yes. Ultramarine? Yes. Sand? Not so much….

I decided what I really wanted was a pair of Uggs the color of crushed raspberries. I mixed three bottles of Wine color dye with one bottle of Neutral (to lighten the color) then dabbed it on with a wool dauber. It took three or four coats. I know that over time I will want to touch it up to re-brighten the color, so I made more dye than needed, labeled the leftovers and stored them in my crafts cupboard.

Cost of materials:
Level of difficulty:
Patience required:

DYEING SUEDE, PAGE 21

A VINTAGE AFFAIR

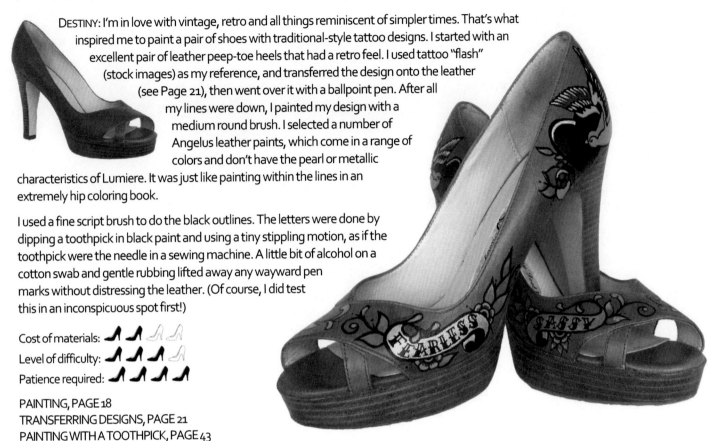

DESTINY: I'm in love with vintage, retro and all things reminiscent of simpler times. That's what inspired me to paint a pair of shoes with traditional-style tattoo designs. I started with an excellent pair of leather peep-toe heels that had a retro feel. I used tattoo "flash" (stock images) as my reference, and transferred the design onto the leather (see Page 21), then went over it with a ballpoint pen. After all my lines were down, I painted my design with a medium round brush. I selected a number of Angelus leather paints, which come in a range of colors and don't have the pearl or metallic characteristics of Lumiere. It was just like painting within the lines in an extremely hip coloring book.

I used a fine script brush to do the black outlines. The letters were done by dipping a toothpick in black paint and using a tiny stippling motion, as if the toothpick were the needle in a sewing machine. A little bit of alcohol on a cotton swab and gentle rubbing lifted away any wayward pen marks without distressing the leather. (Of course, I did test this in an inconspicuous spot first!)

Cost of materials: 👠👠👠👠

Level of difficulty: 👠👠👠👠

Patience required: 👠👠👠👠

PAINTING, PAGE 18
TRANSFERRING DESIGNS, PAGE 21
PAINTING WITH A TOOTHPICK, PAGE 43

PRACTICALLY PAISLEY

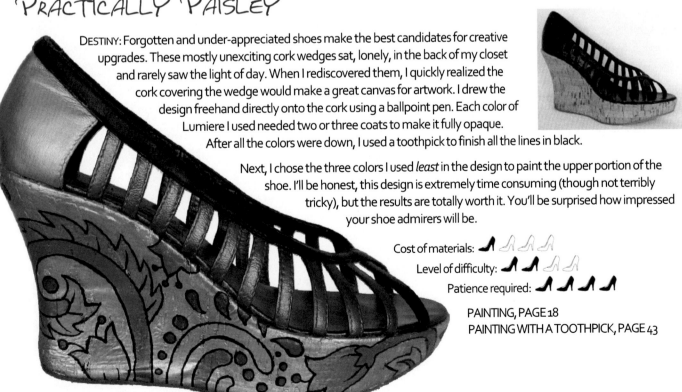

DESTINY: Forgotten and under-appreciated shoes make the best candidates for creative upgrades. These mostly unexciting cork wedges sat, lonely, in the back of my closet and rarely saw the light of day. When I rediscovered them, I quickly realized the cork covering the wedge would make a great canvas for artwork. I drew the design freehand directly onto the cork using a ballpoint pen. Each color of Lumiere I used needed two or three coats to make it fully opaque. After all the colors were down, I used a toothpick to finish all the lines in black.

Next, I chose the three colors I used *least* in the design to paint the upper portion of the shoe. I'll be honest, this design is extremely time consuming (though not terribly tricky), but the results are totally worth it. You'll be surprised how impressed your shoe admirers will be.

Cost of materials: 👠👠👠👠

Level of difficulty: 👠👠👠👠

Patience required: 👠👠👠👠

PAINTING, PAGE 18
PAINTING WITH A TOOTHPICK, PAGE 43

TECHNIQUES USED IN THIS CHAPTER

THE BASICS OF PAINTING SHOES

The single biggest change you can make to transform a shoe is to paint it a different, more interesting or exciting color. Students often ask me, "Won't the color wash off in the rain?" or "Won't it come off on your feet?" or "Won't it peel off?" Not if you follow a few simple rules:

1. Choose the shoes that can be painted
2. Prep the surface of the shoe before painting
3. Use the right paints
4. Seal the paint afterward

CHOOSE THE RIGHT SHOES

You can paint shoes made of leather, suede, manmade leather, manmade suede and most fabrics. Results on patent leather can be dicey, though some people have had luck with it. Just as important, here are the kind of shoes — or parts of shoes — that leather paint *won't* stick to: vinyl, the flexible plastic-like material that Crocs and Croc-alikes (as I call them) are made of, the rubbery plastic soles and decorative "swooshes" on running shoes, and leather shoes that have a water-resistant finish. If you want to paint shoes that are made of stretch fabric, like Lycra, you'll need to use a fabric paint specially formulated for adhering to synthetic, stretchy fabrics. Most people seem to like a product called Jones Tones Fabric & Craft Paints.

PREPPING YOUR SHOES

DON'T SKIP THIS STEP! The reason for prepping the surface of your shoes is get it clean enough for the paint to adhere to it. It doesn't take long to prep shoes and it will make all the difference in how long your paint job lasts. Even if your shoes are brand new, prep them!

You start by stuffing your shoes with newspaper so the surface is smooth and free of wrinkles. Next, apply one of the following, depending on the type of shoe you're working with:

Leather or suede shoes: Wipe the surface with a cotton ball or rag that you've dampened with rubbing alcohol (available at drug stores). Let it dry completely before painting!

Manmade leather shoes: Wipe the surface with a cotton ball or rag that you've dampened with 100% acetone (available at hardware stores; inexpensive). Do this outside as acetone is stinky and not good to inhale. While nail polish remover is acetone too, don't use it to prep your shoes. It could have additives (scent, nail conditioner) that will interfere with the paint's ability to adhere to the shoe. Let it dry completely before painting!

Manmade suede shoes or fabric shoes: Whether your shoes are made of canvas, satin, polyester or manmade suede (which is really polyester), brush them well to remove loose dirt. If they have oil stains, use a stain remover like Kiss-Off (my choice) to get the stains off. Any other type of stains, the paint will simply cover. No need to rub with alcohol or acetone.

THREE WAYS TO TELL LEATHER FROM MANMADE LEATHER

First, leather smells like leather. Second, the materials used to make new shoes must be stamped on them, so look for a sticker on the bottom of the sole or printed information inside the shoe somewhere. Unfortunately, this info has often worn away on older shoes. Third, if you press your fingernail into the surface of the shoe (somewhere that won't be noticed), manmade leather will spring right back, while genuine leather will hold the impression much longer.

A Primer on Leather Paint

We use two brands of acrylic paint for painting shoes: Lumiere and Angelus. Lumiere is what we stock in our Sassy Feet online store, and it's what we use 90% of the time. The instructions below on prepping shoes and sealing them are for use with Lumiere paints. If you choose Angelus paints, which are flatter and come in more traditional shoes colors than Lumiere paints, you will need to purchase their own prep solution and sealer. Angelus products are available from several online stores. Your favorite search engine will find them for you. NOTE: While Lumiere also works on fabric, Angelus is strictly for leather.

All paint for leather (and fabric) is acrylic paint, and here are the basics you need to know about using it on shoes.

- Acrylic paint is water-soluble, which means it can be cleaned up with water as long as it hasn't dried.
- You will probably need two or three coats unless you are painting fabric shoes. The first coat may not look like much, but don't let that discourage you. Also, let each coat dry completely before doing the next coat.
- Acrylic paint dries very quickly. This means you need to keep a container of water at your side to put your brush in when you take a break, even for five minutes.
- Because of this rapid-drying action, don't pour a lot of paint on your palette at one time. If you need to pause while painting (for one coat to dry, or to walk the dog, or even to get a good night's sleep), cover your paint container with plastic wrap. This will keep the paint liquid at least overnight. If the paint gets too gummy, you can dilute it with a little water (don't add more than 25% water).
- Always apply your last coat of paint in broad daylight so you can see the places you missed. No matter how good your shoe looks by indoor light, I guarantee you'll find places you need to touch up once you look at it outdoors.

Fixing Mistakes

If you make a mistake, wipe if off right away with a damp cotton ball, rag or cotton swab. Keep a little cup of clean water by your side just for "erasing" mistakes. If your paint dries and you don't like it, you have three choices:

1. Paint over it. This is by far the best solution!
2. Sand it off with *very* gentle sand paper and then repaint.
3. Paint over a very small part of your mistake at a time, give the paint a moment to penetrate the dried paint beneath it, then gently scrape it away with a hobby knife or your fingernail (which is safer).

Brushes for Applying Paint

First you need something to use as a palette. This could be an actual plastic palette with little wells, a sheet of waxed palette paper, or a Styrofoam plate.

Next come brushes. When you're painting shoes, use *soft* brushes. These will enable you to lay the paint on the surface of the shoe. Make nice smooth strokes, as if you were applying nail polish. We like to use a fan brush, size 1 or 2. We also use a small square-ended brush for painting up to the edges of things, and a small round-pointed brush for painting in tiny places. (We do stock these in our online store.)

Sealing Your Shoes

When you're done painting, you'll need to seal your shoes (unless they are made of fabric or manmade suede). This isn't necessary for most uses of acrylic paint, but shoes live down on the ground where life is rough. They're apt to get scuffed, knocked around, even kicked. So you need a sealer that is tough, clear, and flexible (shoes bend, after all) to protect your paint job.

The sealer that the manufacturer recommends for Lumiere is Pledge with FUTURE Shine Premium Floor Finish. You can buy it in big (27 oz.) bottles at most hardware stores, or in small, inexpensive bottles at www.sassyfeet.com. Apply a light coat with a brush or rag. Wash your brush in soapy water.

COLOR BLOCKING

Color blocking simply means painting different areas in different colors. It's one of the simplest ways to get great shoe-painting results if you think you don't know how to paint. All of the shoes above have been done in some form of color blocking. At right, are the sketches with various areas colored in when Margot was trying to decide what colors to use for her Range Rovers (Page 13

FREESTYLE COLOR BLOCKING

When you're doing color blocking, you don't have to follow the lines of stitching on your shoes or bag. You can fake it! Margot wanted to create a pair of spectator shoes (see Page 14) but didn't want to have to find actual wing tip shoes to work from. So she pressed drafting tape (in this case, cut with pinking shears) over the parts of the shoe to mimic where the stitching would have been. Then she painted the blocked off area, making the final shoe look as if it were composed of two colors of leather stitched together. This is a *very* easy technique!

PAINTING INSOLES

Just as you paint the outside of your shoe, you can paint the inside. Follow the same instructions for prepping, painting and sealing. It really adds the crowning touch to have a sassy or simply freshly painted insole! And no, the paint won't come off on your feet.

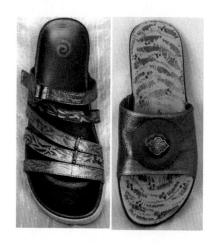

STENCILING

You can use plastic or heavyweight paper stencils to paint images on your shoes, but there are two challenges. First shoes aren't flat, which makes holding the stencil perfectly still and flush against the surface a little tricky. Second, leather and manmade leather don't absorb the paint, like paper and fabric do. What these drawbacks mean is you need a little finesse.

To apply the paint, dab a little on the broad end of a wedge-shaped cosmetic sponge. Don't load up the sponge with paint, though. Just use a little and repeat as needed. I like to dab the sponge once or twice on paper before dabbing over the stencil. This reduces the amount of paint that seeps under the edge of the stencil — which happens because shoes aren't flat and leather isn't absorbent. When your paint dries, be prepared to do touch ups with a small brush to cover up any overflow and fill in any areas that didn't' get enough paint.

There's one other way to use stencils on shoes and bags, which is to tape the stencil in place, then use a contrasting-color pen or paint pen to trace the image onto the surface. Now remove the stencil and fill in the colors you want. This was the technique used on the Cherry Blossom tote in the "Handbags and Bags" chapter.

TRANSFERRING DESIGNS

If you don't think you are artistic enough to paint an image onto your shoes, here's a tip. Find a design you like (and print it out if necessary, or copy it). Do a rough cut around it, and rub the back with chalk in a color that contrasts with the shoe you are painting. Then lay the paper onto the shoe, and trace over the outline with a pencil or pen. This will transfer the chalk onto the shoe and give you a guide with which to paint your outline. The rest is like using a coloring book, just fill in with your desired colors! If the whole idea makes you nervous, practice on scrap material or paper until you get the hang of it.

GLITTERING

One of Margot's most inspired moments was when she devised a way to apply glitter to shoes and handbags in such a way that it didn't crack, peel, or shed tiny sparkly bits all over the place. The product she created is called Glitter It glaze and it can be purchased in our online store. It comes with instructions, but here's how it works. First you paint your shoe a similar color to the color of the glitter you are using. One coat is usually enough, since the Glitter It glaze will cover a multitude of imperfections (making it perfect for using on older, worn shoes and bags!). Once the paint is dry, you mix the glitter packet into the glaze, stir well and apply. Instead of brushing on the Glitter It, you pat it on using a soft fan brush. Be careful not to use too much or the Glitter It glaze will run before it has a chance to dry, which takes about half an hour. Results are fabulous, and you can experiment with glittering your entire shoes, or leaving parts of them just painted.

DYEING SUEDE

We don't recommend painting suede because once you have a coat of paint on it, it loses its softness. If you want to change the color of suede shoes or a bag, use suede dye instead. We like Angelus Suede Dye, which is available online. There are five things you need to know about dyeing suede:

1. You have to take into account the existing color of the shoe when choosing a color of dye. You can only dye things *darker*, not lighter.
2. You can combine colors of dye to get new colors. To lighten a dye color, add Neutral to it.
3. When dyeing, wear latex gloves! Suede dye does not wash off easily.
4. Be prepared to apply three coats of dye to get even coverage: It's hard to get it to absorb evenly.
5. The dye fades over time, so keep your leftover dye in an air-tight jar for use in the future. This is especially important if you mix your own custom color.

CHAPTER 3

ADD A LITTLE SOMETHING

Sometimes all it takes to turn an ordinary shoe into a hand-crafted showpiece is an out-of-this-world embellishment. It could be a big glass bead, a twist of zipper tape, feathers, charms, crystal chain, pearls, big rolled roses, ruffles, appliqués, scraps of beautiful fabric or artfully cut pieces of leather. If you're intimidated by the idea of starting your DIY shoe-design adventures with painting, start by adding embellishments instead.

GALLERY: EMBELLISHED SHOES

TWIST AND SHOUT

MARGOT: One day I looked around and zippers were everywhere! Not just on the backs of dresses or the sides of skirts, but twisted into interesting shapes and worn as brooches, hair ornaments, necklaces, you name it. Having been a longtime sewer, I had quite a stash of zippers, so I pulled out a few and tried it for myself — as an embellishment for a shoe, of course.

I took a long zipper apart and basted along the selvedge of one of the pieces. Then I pulled the thread up tight and knotted it. The zipper comes out in little circles, but you can arrange the gathers so the teeth all show, as in the photo below. Then I tacked my new zipper embellishment to the T-strap of high heel using extra-strong thread (and a leather needle) at top and bottom. I also added a couple of loops from an old pink zipper to make a little flower over the toe, and stitched that down.

Cost of materials: 👠 👠 👠 👠
Level of difficulty: 👠 👠 👠 👠
Patience required: 👠 👠 👠 👠

STITCHING ON EMBELLISHMENTS, PAGE 28

You could position a zipper embellishment in several different places on your shoe. What about across the toe or on the ankle strap?

SPARKLING SIMPLICITY

DESTINY: Over-the-top and bold is usually just what the designer ordered, but there are occasions where dainty and effortless makes just as much of an impact. Since these sandals had such delicate straps, I didn't want to overwhelm their clean lines.

So I chose crystal chain for my embellishment and stitched it across the toe straps. Then I added a sparkling rhinestone button at the top. Draping two more strands of crystal chain created a little extra drama and the finishing touch.

The excellent thing about shoe design is that it doesn't take much, so you can splurge on more expensive embellishments, like fabulous gem chain.

Cost of materials:
Level of difficulty:
Patience required:

STITCHING ON EMBELLISHMENTS, PAGE 28
STITCHING ON CHAIN, PAGE 29

CARMEN MIRANDA SANDALS

MARGOT AND DESTINY: Is there anything sexier on your foot than a strappy little black sandal with a great big lush rose on the toe? How about a multicolored cluster of great big lush roses? And while you're at it, why not add a rose over your ankle, too? Mix up the colors of your roses and make a statement — this is no time to be shy. The result? Our Carmen Miranda Sandals, which were featured in *Altered Couture* magazine.

These rolled roses owe their charm to the fact that they are made of French wired-edge ombre ribbon. Ombre ribbon shifts color from one ribbon edge to the other, which adds depth and mystery. Using wired ribbon pays off in two ways — it makes these roses really easy to gather and roll, and it means that you can change your look from slightly squashed, vintage-looking roses to fresh-from-the garden blooms. TIP: If your ombre ribbon is very dark on one edge and very light on the other, the effect is more striking if you gather the lighter-colored edge and leave the darker-colored edge to form the tips of the "petals."

For instructions on making roses like this, see our blog, glittersweatshop.typepad.com.
The title of the post is "The Last Blooms of Summer."

Cost of materials:
Level of difficulty:
Patience required:

STITCHING ON EMBELLISHMENTS, PAGE 28

23

WAR OF THE ROSES

MARGOT: When I first began reading books and articles about today's top shoe designers, I was surprised to find that the word "witty" kept cropping up in descriptions of their work. Witty. That's "witty" as in quick-witted, intelligent, original, and a little mischievous. This boot aims at wit through its use of cultural contradiction: a sinuous appliqué of twining red roses, gently dangling iridescent glass beads, and 2"-wide hand-dyed silk ribbon, all adorning a Goth-style stomper with eighteen eyelets, two straps, and a platform sole.

"Won't that ribbon break if you use it as shoelaces?" you ask. Good question. The answer is that this boot zips up on the inner-ankle side, so the ribbon laces are purely for looks.

Cost of materials: (appliqué trim can be pricey)
Level of difficulty:
Patience required:

STITCHING ON EMBELLISHMENTS, PAGE 28
GLUING ON TRIM, PAGE 30
SASSIFYING SHOELACES, PAGE 32

WORKING GIRL

MARGOT: So there I was, minding my own business (not thinking about sex at all), just surfing eBay for inexpensive shoes, when I came across an outrageous pair of stiletto-enhanced work boots. My mind boggled. Who had thought

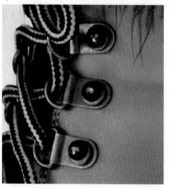

these up? In every way except those killer heels and equally killer toes, these boots were just like the ones my older brothers wore the summer they worked at the steel mill. Honey leather, black padded collar, brass lacing eyes and those classic yellow-and-black laces. A mischievous grin spread across my face — and I started to think of ways to make these boots even more outrageous. The result is Working Girl, complete with black marabou and a little stack of black and topaz rhinestones on each lacing eye.

Cost of materials:
Level of difficulty:
Patience required:

USING FEATHERS, PAGE 32
ATTACHING CRYSTALS, PAGE 31

PEARLY PINK

DESTINY: Suede has a lovely texture, soft and velvety. It takes paint well, but the paint coats the suede, dries hard and smooth, and you lose all the silky nuances that make suede desirable. If you don't like the color of suede, you can dye it with very good results. Luckily, I liked the color of this shoe, and it matched an exquisite length of beaded leaf trim almost perfectly. I wrapped the trim around the collar of the toe, allowing the leaves to extend up beyond the shoe line a bit.

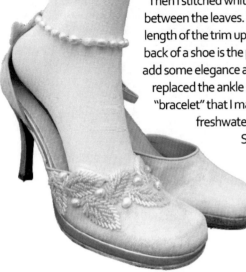

Then I stitched white freshwater pearls zigzagging between the leaves. I also added a short length of the trim up the back seam. The back of a shoe is the perfect place to add some elegance and sass! Finally, I replaced the ankle strap with a "bracelet" that I made from freshwater pearls and pink Swarovski crystals.

Cost of materials: 👠👠👡👡
Level of difficulty: 👠👠👡👡
Patience required: 👠👠👡👡

GLUING ON TRIM, PAGE 30
REPLACING ANKLE STRAPS, PAGE 31

RUFFLES AT MIDNIGHT

MARGOT AND DESTINY: This luxe creation of embellished, dark red ankle booties owes its success to three embellishments — stretchy black ruffles, soutache braid, and an embellishment we made ourselves. Since these booties were already in great condition and came in a wonderful intense color, we elected not to repaint them. Instead, we went "shopping" in Margot's extensively awesome stash. We dug out black spiraly soutache braid (purchased in the bridal department of a lace store!) and a length of multi-tiered stretchy black ruffles (usually used for making tube tops). We glued these on and under the cuff of the bootie. Then we needed a focal point for our design. We dug out of the stash two big black vintage buttons, two hand-hammered copper rings, two white flower-shaped vintage buttons, and two Italian silver swirling buttons. We stacked these up, glued them together and stitched them on the cuff, just in front of the side seam. These shoes have been featured in *Altered Couture* magazine.

Cost of materials: 👠👠👡👡
Level of difficulty: 👠👠👡👡
Patience required: 👠👠👠👡

GLUING ON TRIM, PAGE 30,
STITCHING ON EMBELLISHMENTS, PAGE 28

QUILTER'S COLLAGE

MARGOT: I'd been wanting to do a fabric-collage shoe since I went to a quilting show and noticed that everyone seemed to be wearing black or brown shoes! I thought, these girls need some spicing up! I went to my local quilting store and was a little daunted by the thought of selecting 10-15 different fabrics to create my collage. Then I spotted a little stack of pre-selected and coordinating fabric each cut into a 5" square. It was called a charm pack. Ta-da!

This design uses randomly cut pieces from most of the fabrics in my pack. I used pinking shears to cut decorative edges. Then I got out my trusty fabric glue (see the Sassy Feet Glue Guide on Page 30) and glued the pieces in place, one at a time. I didn't plan it, I just did it! Last of all, I added fold-over elastic binding to protect the fabric at the top edge of the shoe. You'll find complete directions later in this chapter, under Fabric Collage.

Cost of materials:

Level of difficulty:

Patience required:

FABRIC COLLAGE, PAGE 32
ATTACHING PIPING, PAGE

LONNI ROSSI BOOTIE

MARGOT: I felt these little boots deserved something better than manmade suede and big ungraceful laces! So I rooted around in my stash of fabrics and found quite a few small pieces of black, gold and red fabrics designed by Lonni Rossi, who likes Asian motifs and spirals almost as much as I do!

I started cutting strips with my pinking shears, then glued them in place. (For detailed instructions, go to Fabric Collage later in this chapter.) When I came to the toe, I decided to use bigger pieces of fabric and played around gluing, stretching and trimming with my sharp little scissors when the pieces hit the sole line.

I stitched and glued fold-over elastic around the throat of the shoe, then used some of the elastic to replace those boring shoelaces. (I simply inserted it and stitched it together, trusting that the stretch in the elastic would eliminate any need for untying laces.) Finally, I dug out some little brass bells I'd bought at a belly dancing store (I am not making this up), added big black tassels and stitched everything to the top of the laces.

Cost of materials:

Level of difficulty:

Patience required:

FABRIC COLLAGE, PAGE 32
ATTACHING PIPING, PAGE 31
STITCHING ON EMBELLISHMENTS, PAGE 28

KAFFE FASSETT WEDGE

MARGOT: I have this thing about fake wood and fake cork, especially when used on the wedges of shoes. I have a passion for covering it or painting it! I don't think it looks the least little bit like the real thing. I turned to fabric collage — and my favorite fabric designer, Kaffe Fassett — for a solution to these fake stacked-wood wedges. Funny thing is, the solution to covering these wedge came from my UFO pile — you know, that box of Unfinished Objects that all of us who sew (and craft, no doubt) have. This UFO was a quilt block consisting of eight different striped fabrics by Kaffe Fassett. I made a little pattern for the shape of the wedge (for directions on how to do this, see

"Covering Areas With Fabric or Leather" later in this chapter), then placed the pattern over the quilted block so the stripes would be at 45-degree angles. Then I cut and glued and cut some more. It turned out that the wedge curved slightly inward at the heel, so I needed to have a separate narrow, vertical piece to cover that area. When I was done, I glued down some lavender suede cord to cover the raw edges.

Cost of materials:

Level of difficulty:

Patience required:

COVERING AREAS WITH FABRIC OR LEATHER, PAGE 45
FABRIC COLLAGE, PAGE 32
GLUING ON TRIM, PAGE 30

DESERT BOOTS

MARGOT: I love this style of boot so much, I call them YUM boots; I don't think there's anything Ugg-ly about them. This pair seemed like the perfect canvas on which to try out my long-brewing idea to create a genuine desert boot: a boot with a scene of a coyote howling at the full moon while a few backlit clouds drift across the sky. Since I collect scraps of leather the way some people collect parking tickets, I had plenty to sift through looking for colors and textures that would work with this desert landscape.

Destiny drew silhouettes of the cactus, cloud, and coyote for me. (You could also print out desert images — free of copyright, ideally — from the Internet.) I photocopied the silhouettes onto cardstock, cut them out, and used them as patterns for cutting the leather. That's one secret to doing this boot. The other is to use Barge cement. It is ideal for gluing leather to leather, if you follow the directions on the tube.

Cost of materials:

Level of difficulty:

Patience required:

LEATHER COLLAGE, PAGE 32

27

TECHNIQUES USED IN THIS CHAPTER

Here's the most important thing for you to know about attaching embellishment: *Shoes bend but some embellishments don't!* This means that you can't affix a rigid embellishment (like an oversize Asian coin) across an area of your shoe that needs to bend, like the toe.

If you are determined to do this anyway, there are a couple of workarounds. You can mount the embellishment way down on the toe, beyond the line where your foot bends. Or, you can attach the embellishment in such a way that it will move with your foot. For example, you might glue a button back or little leather tab onto the back of your embellishment and stitch that onto your shoe, thus enabling the embellishment to give when you walk.

STITCHING ON EMBELLISHMENTS

Most of the women in our classes want to glue embellishments onto their shoes. For the most part, we convince them not to . Even the best glue can break down over time — especially when subject to all the movement and hard wear that shoes get. So if an embellishment can be stitched on, do it. You don't need to know how to sew, and you certainly don't need a sewing machine. Instead you are going to use a special needle, very strong thread, and a knot that won't come loose.

STITCHING SUPPLIES YOU MUST HAVE

To stitch on embellishments, you'll need:

- **A leather needle** (also called a glover's needle or draper's needle), which has a triangular point. These come in different sizes (i.e., thicknesses). I recommend getting a package that has several different sizes. You want to make as small a hole as possible in the shoe, but you also don't want the needle to bend when you're trying to push it through the leather. They are inexpensive and we carry these in our store.
- **A metal thimble (or a leather thimble with a metal-disc insert) and/or a little pair of pliers** to help push (and pull) the needle through the leather. I use both when I'm stitching.
- **Thread that won't break or fray over time.** My first choice is always FireLine or DandyLine beading thread. You can also use nylon upholstery thread, but it's a lot bulkier. Available at beading stores or online.

HOW TO TIE A KNOT THAT WILL REALLY STAY TIED

When you are stitching on an embellishment, the last thing you want to have to worry about is whether it will fly off one day when you are running to catch a cab. That's why I recommend using unbreakable beading thread and tying the right kind of knot — one that won't work loose as you walk, run, jump, skip, and kick the tires of your stalled car.

The right knot is the kind surgeons use. It's just like a square knot (the one that's usually explained as "Right over left, then left over right"), except that you make an extra "right over left" before pulling the first half of the knot tight. That extra pass prevents your thread from loosening while you're tying the second half of the knot (the "left over right" part).

We always use TWO surgeon's knots just to be safe. The picture below shows how to tie ONE surgeon's knot.

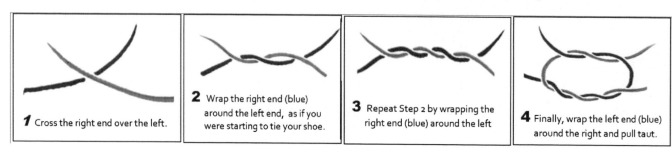

1 Cross the right end over the left.

2 Wrap the right end (blue) around the left end, as if you were starting to tie your shoe.

3 Repeat Step 2 by wrapping the right end (blue) around the left

4 Finally, wrap the left end (blue) around the right and pull taut.

The Secrets of Successful Stitching

Three things are *critical* when you are stitching on embellishments.

1. Use a double or even quadruple strand of FireLine or DandyLine beading thread. (I use a quadruple strand so I don't have to take a lot of stitches.)
2. Don't knot your thread on the inside of the shoe where it can rub against your tender feet. Instead, knot it on the outside of the shoe, but underneath the embellishment (so the knot doesn't show).
3. Knot your thread with a double surgeon's knot, which won't come undone over time.

How to Stitch on Embellishments

We are going to explain this step by step. It isn't complicated, it just looks that way from the number of steps! It will help a lot if you have a needle, thread and piece of scrap fabric (as a stand-in for your shoe) when you read these steps. That way you can do the steps with your hands, not just in your head, and you'll see that they are pretty straightforward.

1. Cut a long enough piece of thread so that when it's doubled (or quadrupled), you will have enough to stitch down your embellishment and an extra 8" for easily tying your surgeon's knot.
2. Don't try to make a knot in the end of the thread like you would if you were sewing on a button. Leave the thread unknotted. Begin by sinking your leather needle into the outside of your shoe, just underneath where your embellishment will be.
3. Pull the needle through to the inside of your shoe, leaving a tail on the outside that's 4" long. This tail will be one of the two ends you'll use to make your finishing knot.
4. Push the needle back up through the shoe, this time going from the inside to the outside.
5. Now loop your needle and thread through your embellishment and sink the needle back into the shoe again. Pull it taut on the inside. Proceed this way until you have your embellishment secure.
6. When you are ready to tie your knot, you need to end up with your needle on the *outside* of your shoe, but *underneath* your embellishment. That's where the beginning tail of your thread is, just waiting politely to be knotted off. This will give you two ends of thread with which to tie your surgeon's knots. Tie TWO knots.
7. Leave your thread tails long. One at a time, thread them back in your needle and take a few stitches to bury them invisibly in your shoe or embellishments. If you can't do that, at least don't clip the threads right at the knot. Even a surgeon's knot will come untied if you snip the tails off too close to it.

Stitching on Chain

We love using chain on our shoes, whether it's purely for decoration or serves a functional purpose (like replacing a leather ankle and T-strap). Chain needs to be stitched on so that it won't pop loose when you walk. The catch is that each link in a chain also has a tiny opening where the ends of the metal were bent to form the link and you need to be sure that opening isn't so big that your thread slips through.

If that's the case, slide a split ring onto the link of the chain and stitch that to your shoe. Or you can make a little leather or elastic "tab" (a narrow loop) and stitch that down.

Gluing on Embellishments

Yes, you *can* glue certain embellishments onto shoes. If the embellishment is flexible, such as an appliqué, glue will work great. If your embellishment is *not* flexible (such a metal charm), glue will work great if you are attaching the embellishment to a part of the shoe that won't bend or flex when you walk.

Equally important is that you have to use the right glue. The right glue is the kind that dries clear and flexible, and is specifically formulated to work on *both* of the materials you are gluing together. On the next page is a guide to the brands that work best for us in different situations. You may get different results or prefer another product. There are a lot of variables that affect the success of a particular glue in a particular situation. Whichever type or brand you choose, read and follow its directions. Don't take it on trust that it will do what the fine print says. Test it first on similar materials to those you'll be gluing!

The Notorious Sassy Feet Glue Guide

To glue this:	To this:	We like to use this:
Fabric trim or piping	Unpainted leather	Fabri-Tac glue
Fabric trim or piping	Unpainted manmade materials	The Ultimate glue by Crafter's Pick
Fabric trim or piping	Unpainted fabric	Fabri-Tac glue
Fabric trim or piping	Painted surfaces, whether leather, manmade materials or fabric	The Ultimate glue
Anything with an uneven surface, where you need the glue to fill the gaps	Any materials	E6000 and clamp for 24 full hours – or stitch or wire on the embellishment.
Leather	Unpainted leather	Barge Cement
Leather	Painted leather	527 Bond
Beads	Anything	Don't glue them stitch them on
Metal charms, stampings, chains, or other metal embellishments	Any surface	I prefer to stitch them on, but if I must glue them, I use either 527 Bond (which dries quickly) or E6000 (which I clamp for 24 hours)
Crystals	Fabric	Gemtac or hot-fix

Note: I don't use super glue, because it stains fabric and it's not flexible. It also destroys the foil backing on Swarovski flatback crystals.

Supplies to Help You Glue

In addition to using the right glue, your success (and good mood) will depend on having a few other supplies on hand:

- Glue applicators (inexpensive little squeeze bottles with very narrow tips), so you can apply very thin lines of glue and not wear out your hands squeezing big bottles. (We have these in our online store.)
- Mini spring clamps for holding embellishments in place while the glue dries
- A piece of aluminum foil for holding a dollop of glue that you're going to apply with a toothpick
- Toothpicks for poking glue into tiny spaces or shoving tiny embellishments into place.
- Rags for wiping off any overflowing glue
- Something to protect your table from glue (I use old magazines; you can also buy a glue or adhesive mat.)

How To Glue On Embellishments

Spread glue on the embellishment. Position it on your shoe. If needed, clamp it into place until it dries. Above all, use the right glue for the two materials you are gluing together and follow the directions on the glue's packaging!

Gluing on Trim

One of the nice things about attaching trim to your shoes is that because it is made of fabric, it will bend when the shoe bends. Use the Sassy Feet Glue Guide above to decide which glue to use. Squeeze a little at a time on your trim and press it into place. If you are using Fabri-Tac, it is sticky enough that you won't need to clamp the trim. If you are using The Ultimate, you may need to clamp or hold the trim in place for a few minutes until the glue gets tacky as it begins to dry.

Once all the trim is glued down and the glue is dry, take a toothpick and try to lift up the edges of the trim. If anything seems loose, apply more glue, using a toothpick to push the glue under the loose edge of the trim

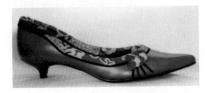

ATTACHING PIPING

Piping is a narrow fabric trim or ribbon that you put around the throat of a shoe. You can glue it in place (see the Sassy Feet Glue Guide on Page 30 for which glue to use) as long as you stitch the points where the trim begins and ends. We like to start and end our trim on the part of the shoe just above the inner ankle. This is the least noticeable part of a shoe.

Once you have your piping glued down and it has dried, test it by pulling it at various points. If anything seems loose, apply more glue, using a toothpick to push the glue under the loose edge of the piping.

ATTACHING CRYSTALS

We women seem to love wearing sparkly little crystals on our clothes! Can you put them on shoes and expect them to stick? The answer is, sometimes. Here are two ways you can successfully glue or (hot-fix) crystals onto shoes

1. Glue them to a part of the shoe that won't bend. Otherwise, the flexing of the shoe's surface when you walk will cause those little puppies to pop off! We use Gemtac for this.
2. Glue, hot-fix or iron them onto fabric that you will glue onto the shoe. For example, on the hightop we made for Ellen DeGeneres (Page 41), we glued the blue zircon crystals to white Ultrasuede using Gemtac, then glued the Ultrasuede onto the toe of her sneaker using Flip Flop Glue. On the Pirate Girl bag (Page 54), we used an iron-on crystal motif, applying it to black fabric, cutting away the extra material, then gluing the crystal skull and crossbones onto the front of the bag.

ADDING ANKLE TIES

You can add an ankle tie to a shoe by gluing or stitching a narrow little loop of ribbon, leather or Ultrasuede to the inside of the back seam. Ankle ties can also start nearer the front of the shoe, cross the instep and go through loops (which you have made) near the ankle, then up around the ankle as many times as you choose. How long do ankle ties need to be? They can be as long as you want them to be. In general, ties that anchor at the back seam and go around your ankle once are 14-18" each.

REPLACING ANKLE STRAPS

If you want to add a bit of spice to shoes with ankle straps, replace those straps with chain, beading or ribbon. Usually you can simply slide out the existing strap and slide in or stitch down your new one. If you want to make a beaded strap, you construct it as you would a bracelet, using a large lobster-claw or toggle clasp.

If the existing strap is stitched onto your shoe, you can cut it off, leaving long ends that you can use to make loops for anchoring your new strap. (Stitch the loops closed, don't just glue them.) If your new "strap" is a chain, use split rings to make the connection between the chain and your leather loops.

SASSIFYING YOUR SHOELACES

There are several things you can do to make the laces on your shoes sassier! If the laces aren't actually functional because the shoe or boot zips closed, go to town! Use silk ribbon, lace or delicate chain. It won't matter, because it's purely decorative. If your laces have to be functional, you can still use ribbon if it's strong, or if you buy several extra lengths to use when it wears out. Last of all, if you have a sewing machine, you can do decorative stitching on your laces using a topstitching needle and thread in the needle *and* the bobbin. As one student told us, "This was worth the price of the class!"

USING FEATHERS

Feathers can be stitched or glued to shoes, depending what form them come in. Easiest to use are feather pads, where individual feathers have already been glued to a teardrop-shaped piece of fabric. This pad can be glued to the side of a boot or stitched down (if it will be on a part of the shoe that will bend). Loose feathers and boas can be stitched down.

FABRIC COLLAGE

Choose 8-10 patterns (or solids) of tightly woven fabrics like high-quality quilting material. Spray only as much fabric as you are going to need with stain-proofing like Scotch-Gard Fabric & Upholstery Protector. Now, using pinking shears, cut out strips or random shapes. For the edges that will meet the sole line, use straight scissors.

Consult the Sassy Feet Glue Guide on Page 30 to determine which glue to use. To glue down a strip, apply a little glue to one end of the strip on the wrong side of the fabric, and press the strip into place, starting at the back of the shoe. The end should sit right at the sole line. Use your fingernail to press the edge of the fabric into the seam at the sole line, if possible.

Working from bottom to top, apply more glue (just a little will do) to the very edges of the strip and press them down, working all the way up to the top of the shoe. When the strip is glued, trim the top even with the top of your shoe.

Choose another strip of fabric and repeat the process, overlapping the pinked edge of the first strip by just a little. Continue to work this way on both sides of the shoe until you are getting near the point where the toe of the shoe begins. Now you have a design decision to make. If you want to continue creating a random or

> ### RESTRAIN YOURSELF!
> The more glue you use, the stiffer your fabric will be when the glue dries. Use just enough glue to do the job, no more. You can always add more later if you need to.

stripped patchwork, keep going until the shoe is covered. If you'd rather emphasize the toe area by using just two or three fabrics, cut larger shapes and glue them in the same way. The only difference is, when working on the toe of the shoe, glue the *top edge* of each shape first and work down toward the toe of the shoe.

When you're done and the glue is dry, take a toothpick and see if you can lift any of the glued edges of your strips. If so, use a toothpick to push a little glue under the loose edge. Finally, put on piping or fold-over elastic trim to protect the top edge of the collage from the friction caused when you slip your foot in and out of the shoe. See ATTACHING PIPING, Page 31.

You can also use fabric collage to cover the wedge of a shoe, as on the Kaffe Fassett wedge. For directions on making a pattern in the shape of your wedge, see Covering Areas With Fabric or Leather, Page 45.

LEATHER COLLAGE

Cut out your leather shapes and glue them into place (see the Sassy Feet Glue Guide on Page 30) and following the directions on the packaging. Remember that faux suede boots are actually made of fabric. When you're done and the glue is dry, take a toothpick and see if you can lift any of the glued edges of your leather pieces. If so, use a toothpick to push a little glue under the loose edge.

Photo by Bobbi Bullard

Shoes painted and embellished during a one-day class by members of the American Sewing Guild's Gold Country chapter

CHAPTER 4
PUTTING IT ALL TOGETHER

Now we're cooking! The shoes in this chapter use both aspects of DIY shoe design: painting and embellishing. Some are painted and embellished to the hilt, others are more restrained (though just as appealing). You'll see how the two sets of skills work together on these shoes to create some wonderful effects — and truly one-of-a-kind shoes!

GALLERY: PAINTED AND EMBELLISHED SHOES

FAN DANCE

MARGOT: If I don't have an idea already in mind when I set out to create a DIY shoe design, I use one of two approaches. Either I start with a color of paint I LOVE, or I start with an embellishment I LOVE. I found these gorgeous little green fans of woven lamé in a very unusual store in Berkeley, California, called Castle in the Air. I bought six of them. At the time, I wasn't sure how I'd use them on shoes, but once I got them home, inspiration struck. I painted these flats in Sunset Gold, then used big glass beads to anchor the fans in place. (I had "auditioned" the placement of these embellishments using earthquake putty, aka poster putty to those of you who don't live where the ground shakes from time to time.) Simple, but very fetching!

Cost of materials:
Level of difficulty:
Patience required:

PAINTING, PAGE 18
STITCHING ON EMBELLISHMENTS, PAGE 28

33

ANCIENT SPIRALS

MARGOT: In native cultures all over the world, the spiral symbolizes transformation. It's a theme — and a shape — I've been fascinated with all my life. I learned about the meaning of spirals from Angeles Arrien in *Signs of Life*, a book on the five universal shapes and what they mean. Arrien is also known for her work teaching people how to "walk the mystical path with practical feet," a perfect concept for those of us who love to create shoes that express who we are inside as well as outside.

These slippers were painted Citrine then stamped with a variety of spirals, using various shades of Lumiere instead of stamping ink. Last, I stitched spiral charms around the front, anchoring each spiral with a tiny glass bead. (To be honest, when I first did these shoes, early on in my shoe-embellishing career, I glued on the spiral charms — and they popped right off! The flexing of the shoe was too much for the glue. So I went back and stitched instead. Live and learn!)

Rubber stamps © Purrfectly Clear
www.danamarie.com

Cost of materials:
Level of difficulty:
Patience required:

PAINTING, PAGE 18
STAMPING, PAGE 44
STITCHING ON EMBELLISHMENTS, PAGE 28

OLD-FASHIONED GIRL

MARGOT: I love taking a traditional design and giving it a little nontraditional pizzazz. In the case of this wingtip boot, I used a technique called color blocking, a fancy name for painting different clearly marked-off sections of an object in different colors. Here I painted over two of the once-black sections with a gleaming Metallic Russet and a more muted shade of Crimson tinted with a drop or two of Neopaque Black. A double strand of copper chain hangs freely from one side, stitched on using tiny leather tabs. It curves below a little copper butterfly in flight, glued onto the leather in a part of the shoe that won't flex and bend a lot. . The crowning touch is a wide ombre ribbon shot through with copper lamé that serves as a shoelace.

Cost of materials:
Level of difficulty:
Patience required:

PAINTING, PAGE 18
COLOR BLOCKING PAGE 20
STITCHING ON CHAIN , PAGE 29
GLUING ON EMBELLISHMENTS, PAGE 29
SASSIFYING YOUR SHOELACES, PAGE 32

34

FANDANGO

MARGOT: This boot started out solid black, but the alternating shades of black and rust in its stacked heel tempted me to find a way to mix those shades in the boot itself. What I came up with was to paint the boot with Metallic Rust, then antique it (by wiping on Neopaque Black — small sections at a time — and very quickly wiping off most of it. Next I stitched an inexpensive cluster of pheasant feathers (which is called a feather pad and comes already mounted on a fabric backing) to the side of the boot. On top of that, I glued an eye-catching beaded medallion. Suddenly that plain black boot wasn't so plain anymore! These sassy boots have been featured in *Altered Couture* magazine.

Cost of materials:

Level of difficulty:

Patience required:

PAINTING, PAGE 18
ANTIQUING, PAGE 43
USING FEATHERS, PAGE 32
STITCHING ON
    EMBELLISHMENTS, PAGE 28

Though I'm grateful for the blessings of wealth, it hasn't changed who I am.

My feet are still on the ground — I'm just wearing better shoes.

OPRAH

FRINGE BENEFITS

MARGOT: What's your great-grandmother's cameo doing dangling from a boot? Making a fashion statement, that's what. Actually, I found the cameo and its setting at a bead store. The trim around the top of the boot is confetti fringe, so called because it has tiny squares of chenille on each 3" strand of fringe. Since it's made of 100 percent polyester, it's inexpensive and impervious to rain. (And it looks a lot like feather trim, which is neither!) I also sponged blue and silver paint over the originally black boot to dress it up a bit. These booties have been featured in *Altered Couture* magazine.

Cost of materials:

Level of difficulty:

Patience required:

PAINTING, PAGE 18
DILUTE PAINTING, PAGE 43
STITCHING ON EMBELLISHMENTS, PAGE 28
GLUING ON TRIM, PAGE 30

BAUBLES AND BEADS

MARGOT: I was scrolling through Zappos.com one day, looking at one of the Buyer's Favorites selections, when I spotted a wonderful detail on a sandal by Kenzo. He'd used jingle bells clustered with silver-tone corrugated beads. I decided to go one better by adding a variety of gold-toned and copper corrugated beads and a single dyed freshwater pearl. This mix of colors served to inspire me to paint multicolor metallic straps—five different shades on the toe straps, ankle strap and heel. (By the way, those Kenzo sandals had a $300 price tag, and that was five years ago!)

TIP: When painting narrow, close-set straps in different colors, separate them so you can easily paint one color at a time. Pieces snipped from a cosmetic wedge will hold the straps apart while you paint.

Cost of materials:

Level of difficulty:

Patience required:

PAINTING, PAGE 18 — COLOR BLOCKING, PAGE 20 — STITCHING ON EMBELLISHMENTS, PAGE 28

BLUE HAIKU

MARGOT: How can the East symbolize so many different things to us Westerners? Luxurious gold-embroidered kimonos, spare haiku. Elaborate ceremonies, restrained manners. Maybe the contrasts are what fascinate us so. Whatever the reason, I fell in love with the style of the East when I was in college, and it's a love affair that's lasted.

Silk is synonymous with the Far East, so when I found brightly printed silk bias binding, I knew I had to use it on an Asian-themed shoe. I painted the leather in Pearlescent Blue to bring out the blue in the silk print. Then I added narrow black faux-suede trim to the outer edge of the binding to highlight its effect. Last of all, I stitched four Asian charms and some little strips of the black faux-suede trim as a focal point. This shoe is one of our most popular, so we created a kit for it, complete with paint, bias tape, Ultrasuede trim, charms, and detailed instructions. Just add shoes!

Cost of materials:

Level of difficulty:

Patience required:

PAINTING, PAGE 18
ATTACHING PIPING, PAGE 31
GLUING ON TRIM, PAGE 30

TASTE OF THE TROPICS

MARGOT: At the beginning of each class, I do a demo on how to paint, showing the students how to brush on the Lumiere paint gently and smoothly. You do it with just a few strokes, as if you were putting on nail polish. One day, I was using a pair of Cole Haan leather slides that a stylish friend had handed-me-down as the demo shoe. It was a lush tropical green that reminded me of Hawaii. I chose Metallic Copper to paint the upper, which was a great contrast. Usually, that's where I stop when I do a demo.

But as the day went on, this group of artisans didn't need a lot of help from me, so I picked up my brush and kept playing around with the shoe. I painted the underside of the upper in Metallic Olive Green. Then I put my nearly worn-out fan brush (it had gotten sort of spiky over time!) to good use. It looked to me like the fan with its slightly spayed bristles might make interesting shapes on the insole of the shoe. So I dipped it in Metallic Olive Green and started pressing it in little arcs. This took a little chutzpah, because I had no idea how it would look -- and what if it came out terrible and all my students saw what a mess I'd created?

I've always been a risk-taker, though, so I plunged ahead. Luckily, I liked the effect! The brush marks looked like palm fronds. I decided to paint little berries onto the fronds (not sure why, it's holly that has berries -- just consider it artistic license). I used Metallic Bronze daubed with Metallic Rust for the berries. Fine. But class wasn't over yet and still no one needed a lot of help from me! So I added some detail on the top and bottom edge of the upper, again using the spikiness of my old fan brush to create interesting patterns.

When I got home, I put together an embellishment by gluing together a large resin doughnut, a smaller metal donut and a gold-tone button. I just wish it were in my size, instead of my stylish friend's size 6!

Cost of materials: 👠👠
Level of difficulty: 👠👠
Patience required: 👠👠

PAINTING, PAGE 18
PAINTING PIPING, PAGE 43
PAINTING INSOLES, PAGE 20
STITCHING ON EMBELLISHMENTS, PAGE 28

BROCADE DREAMS

MARGOT: One of the easiest ways to make a plain shoe look customized is to add piping around the throat. Here, I've used a length of lush brocade piping so thick it must have been made for interior decorators to use on the seams of fancy pillows. I also wrapped the piping across the vamp from sole line to sole line, creating the appearance of a seam where none really exists. Four narrow rows of matching silk cord set off the faux seam line, and a nicely wrought brass stamping provided the finishing touch.

Cost of materials: 👠👠
Level of difficulty: 👠👠
Patience required: 👠👠👠

PAINTING, PAGE 18
ATTACHING PIPING, PAGE 31
GLUING ON TRIM, PAGE 30
STITCHING ON EMBELLISHMENTS, PAGE 28

OUT OF THIS WORLD

MARGOT: On a recent blog, Destiny and I dubbed this shoe "most improved." It was not that the original shoe was awful, but in person it felt an awfully lot like plastic and didn't quite carry off its retro look. I started by cutting the threads that stitched the bow in place. Then I looked at the shoe anew. It seemed to me that the stitching lines called for color blocking, but what if ... I color-blocked it with our Glitter It glaze?

I painted undercoats of silver and black on the different areas, then dabbed on two coats of Sparkling Silver and Starlet Glitter It glaze. It looked good, but it wasn't ... enough. In DIY shoe design, it almost always pays to go one, sometimes two, steps further. So, I painted the lining of the shoe Super Copper. An interesting thing happened while I was doing that: I slopped over the edges a bit and the copper showed on the outside of the shoe -- and it looked great! Because of the texture in the glitter, the result was a nice smudgy edge, which seemed to work well. Then I painted the insole itself black, to provide more contrast.

At this point I thought the shoes looked fine and was going to stop messing with them. But then I went to a bead store that sold dichroic glass and fell in love with a couple of little pieces. I made my own embellishment out of two little lozenges and an open square, by gluing them together with E6000 and attaching a button back so I could stitch it on.

Cost of materials:
Level of difficulty:
Patience required:

PAINTING, PAGE 18
GLITTERING, PAGE 21
PAINTING PIPING, PAGE 43
STITCHING ON EMBELLISHMENTS , PAGE 28

ORCHID SUNSET

MARGOT: The idea for this shoe originated with some delicious tangerine-and-amethyst hand-dyed silk ribbon I found at an online trim store (mjtrim.com). Once it arrived, I ran it through my fingers again and again, fascinated by the color shift from bright orange to deep violet. I started wondering if I could paint a shoe with that kind of effect. It turned out surprisingly easy to do. The toe is Burnt Orange, the center is Halo Violet Gold, and the heel is Pearlescent Violet, with lots of light cosmetic-sponge dabbing in between. (Instructions are on Page 43.) After painting, I attached the ribbon so it crisscrossed the instep like the ribbon on a ballet slipper and tied around the ankle.

Cost of materials:
Level of difficulty:
Patience required:

PAINTING, PAGE 18
PAINTING COLOR TRANSITIONS, PAGE 43
ADDING ANKLE TIES, PAGE 31

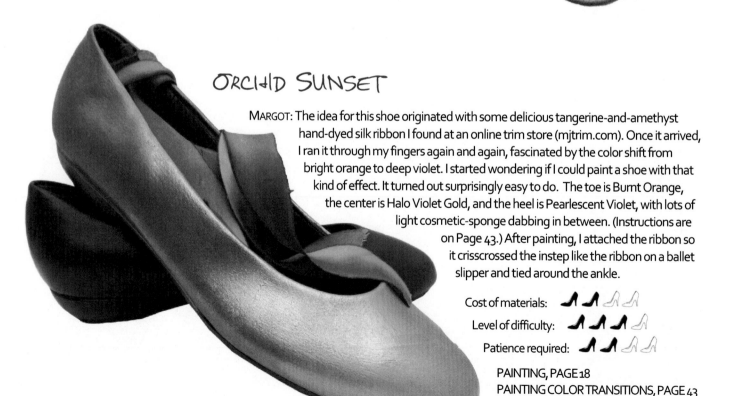

GOOD MORNING, PARIS

MARGOT: Ballet shoes, like animal prints, seem to be continually in style. They're cute, they're comfortable — and they make even my feet (size 9) look petite. What's not to like? This little slipper adds a French flair to its already charming look. A white enamel plaque greets all who see it, and a miniature Eiffel Tower swings gaily from the heel. Scattered across a field of Pearlescent Magenta are tiny white fleurs-de-lis, the ancient symbol of the French monarchy. Because I love the shape of fleurs-de-lis but can't draw worth a dam, I had to come up with a way to paint them that required no artistic talent. I call it Reverse Stenciling and the instructions are later in this chapter.

Cost of materials:

Level of difficulty:

Patience required:

PAINTING, PAGE 18
REVERSE STENCILING, PAGE 44
ATTACHING PIPING, PAGE 31
STITCHING ON EMBELLISHMENTS , PAGE 28

LETTERS FROM HOME

MARGOT: Hurrah for scrapbookers! Thanks to them, there are lots of stores (online and off) filled with cool charms and doodads of all sorts that you can use to decorate shoes. (Just DON'T choose ones made of paper — they won't last!) This sandal is painted lightly in Metallic Rust and embellished with bracelet links created by a marvelous little company called 7 Gypsies. I used two different collections of their links, one that includes the words hope, dream, create, love, friend, and home, and another that says (in a seductive French accent) *ami, adore, vie, chic, merci,* and *petit.* A final bit of sass comes from saucy little bows of red rayon yarn that appear to tie the bracelet links to the shoe. (In reality, those links are securely anchored by FireLine beading thread.) These sandals have been featured in *Altered Couture.*

Note: We have created a kit with everything you need to make these sandals (except the shoes!), or you can buy just the bracelet links from us at store.sassyfeet.com.

Cost of materials:

Level of difficulty:

Patience required:

PAINTING, PAGE 18
SEA SPONGING, PAGE 44
STITCHING ON EMBELLISHMENTS , PAGE 28

Don't follow trends — follow yourself. You have to stand tall and proud.

Manolo Blahnik

Pretty in Pink

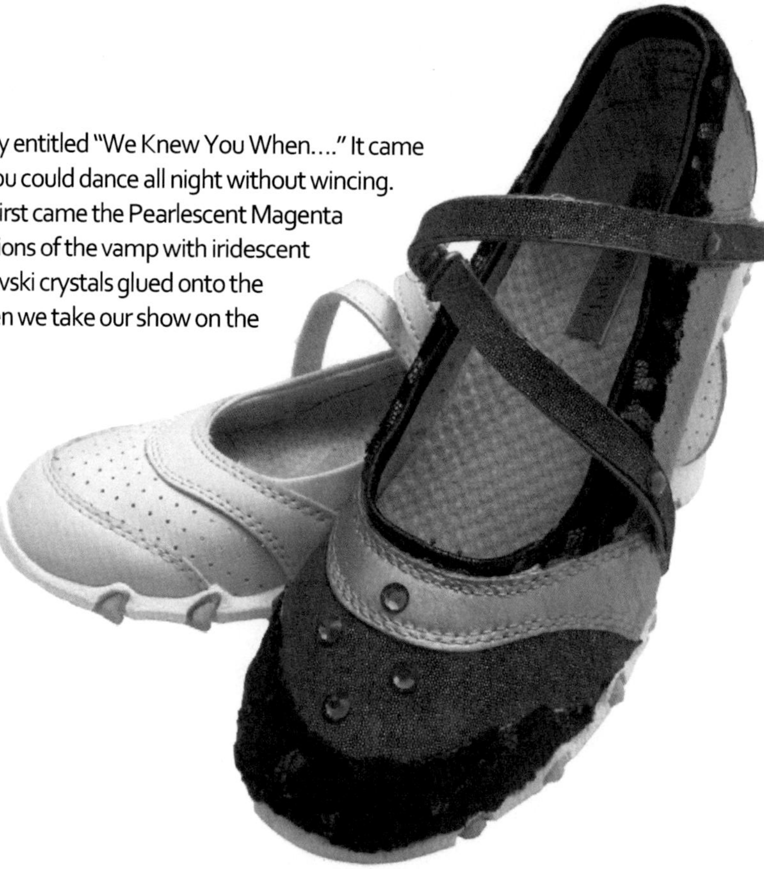

MARGOT: This shoe should probably have its own category entitled "We Knew You When...." It came about because I wanted to create a party shoe in which you could dance all night without wincing. So I started with a comfy sport shoe and experimented. First came the Pearlescent Magenta paint. Then I glued on stretchy black lace and filled in sections of the vamp with iridescent leather. The final touch? A handful of big magenta Swarovski crystals glued onto the leather. This is one of the shoes women exclaim over when we take our show on the road!

Cost of materials:
Level of difficulty:
Patience required:

PAINTING, PAGE 18
COVERING AREAS WITH FABRIC OR LEATHER, PAGE 45
ATTACHING PIPING, PAGE 31
ATTACHING CRYSTALS, PAGE 31

In the Coral Jungle

MARGOT: Does one really need to embellish a pair of leopard stilettos to make them sexy? Not if she doesn't mind them looking like everyone else's leopard stilettos. But if you want to make a statement — and catch a certain someone's eye — then try this. First tint them pink using a diluted version of Pearlescent Magenta (which, when applied over the tawny leopard skin background, creates a coral shade). Then paint a line of faux piping with full-strength Pearlescent Magenta. To top it off, wrap up the heel and ankle with a wide ribbon of coral-tinged organza tied off with Bali silver beads. You can anchor it at the top of the back seam by threading a medium-large split ring onto a narrow strip of leather and stitching or gluing down the ends, making a little loop. Thread the ribbon through that loop, and there you are.

Cost of materials:
Level of difficulty:
Patience required:

PAINTING, PAGE 18
DILUTE PAINTING, PAGE 43
PAINTING PIPING, PAGE 43
ADDING ANKLE TIES, PAGE 31

DIVA COUTURE

DESTINY: This shoe started out as a plain white bridal heel. I began by painting it Pearlescent Magenta, then slathering on all the Petal Pink Glitter It glaze that any diva — or showgirl — could desire. Next I painted pin stripes down the heel and wider strips on the insole for a couture touch. On the toe, I stitched down a cluster of German cut-crystal drops topped with a rhinestone button. Last of all, I glued a line of flatback rhinestones down the back seam. For tips on how to do these steps, check out the instructions referenced below. These heels were featured in *Altered Couture* magazine.

Cost of materials:

Level of difficulty:

Patience required:

PAINTING, PAGE 18
GLITTERING, PAGE 21
PAINTING STRIPES, PAGE 44
ATTACHING CRYSTALS, PAGE 31
STITCHING ON EMBELLISHMENTS , PAGE 28

ESPECIALLY ELLEN

MARGOT AND DESTINY: We created these personalized high tops for Ellen DeGeneres in her favorite shades of blue. We started with a pair of royal blue Converse sneakers and dabbed on a custom color of Glitter It glaze. We chose *not* to glitter the areas around the metal grommets or the vertical section at the very back.

Our best inspiration was to make little patterns of the sneaker toes, cut out pieces of white Ultrasuede, then glue blue zircon Swarovski crystals onto them. (If we'd tried gluing them directly onto the rubber toe, they would have popped off the moment Ellen took her first step.) We glued these to the toes using Flip Flop glue, which *does* stick to rubbery surfaces. The finishing touch was to use a toothpick and Glitter It glaze to paint capital E's — in Ellen's handwriting — over the rubber circles with the Converse logo.

Cost of materials:

Level of difficulty:

Patience required:

GLITTERING, PAGE 21
ATTACHING CRYSTALS, PAGE 31
PAINTING WITH A TOOTHPICK, PAGE 43

STERLING STEAMPUNK

DESTINY: These are shoes fit for a (time-traveling, sterling-silver steampunk) princess! I covered the plastic straw wedge with silver and copper leafing, which is easier to apply than you might think. The blue-plaid fabric upper got a coat of rich matte Neopaque Black. For an extra steampunk touch, I decorated the insoles by painting them Pewter and adding hand-painted gears in Metallic Russet. The embellishment on the toe is a button that Margot had in her stash, highlighted by a single sparkling Swarovski crystal.

Cost of materials:

Level of difficulty:

Patience required:

PAINTING, PAGE 18
STITCHING ON EMBELLISHMENTS, PAGE 28
METALLIC LEAFING, PAGE 45

GLITTERATI

MARGOT AND DESTINY: Five shades of Glitter It glaze swirl across the surface of what began as a plain black Mary Jane pump. This was an idea Margot dreamed up, the drawback to which was that Destiny had to design the swirl pattern and color combinations — and then had to paint an undercoat in the same patterns (and in multiple colors). But she made Margot apply the glitter! Margot got her revenge by "offering" to teach Destiny how to paint silk. Destiny fought back by mixing colors and applying them perfectly! Margot took the painted silk charmeuse, cut it into bias strips, made rolled roses and stitched them on the straps. It looked pretty good but needed one more little touch — like metallic silver lace peeking out from the edge of the vamp. At this point, we both retired from the fray, victorious! These shoes were chosen to appear in the acclaimed Wearable Expressions exhibit in Los Angeles, less than one year after we started doing shoes together!

Cost of materials:

Level of difficulty:

Patience required:

PAINTING, PAGE 18
GLITTERING, PAGE 21
GLUING ON EMBELLISHMENTS, PAGE 29
STITCHING ON EMBELLISHMENTS, PAGE 28

ADDITIONAL TECHNIQUES USED IN THIS CHAPTER

PAINTING COLOR TRANSITIONS

This technique is surprisingly easy. It just requires patience. Paint the heel (or whatever area) what we'll call Color A. Paint the toe (or whatever other area) Color B. Now mix small amounts of the two colors together in different proportions, on three different places on your palette. Using a wedge-shaped cosmetic sponge, *lightly* sponge on these mixtures, blotting the color-loaded sponge a couple times first on your palette to get any excess paint off. Working from dark to light until you get something that looks like a fairly smooth color transition. Remember, shoes are worn at least four feet away from any adults' eyes, so the transition doesn't have to be 100% perfect. (If you are transitioning between two colors that will turn a completely different color when mixed, skip the mixing and just keep lightly sponging, letting it dry, and lightly sponging some more.

PAINTING PIPING

You can paint "piping" onto the edges of your shoe instead of gluing down fabric piping. It takes a little patience to get the painted edge even, but the results are impressive. You can also use a nearly dry fan brush to stroke on a contrasting color, dabbing the paint away from the area you are painting so the bristles of the brush leaves a nice irregular edge like the one on copper colored sandal. For a larger photo of this, see Taste of the Tropics on Page 37.

DILUTE PAINTING

Lumiere paint can be diluted up to 25% with water if you want to get watercolor effects or let the original color of the shoe come through, as Margot did on In the Coral Jungle , Page 40. You can also leave the paint full strength but dab on light layers of it using a wedge-shaped cosmetic sponge and blotting the color-loaded sponge first on your palette to get any excess paint off. You can even use different colors while doing this for the kind of effect used on Fringe Benefits, Page 35.

ANTIQUING

You can get an antiqued look on smooth leather or manmade leather by wiping on a light coat of Neopaque Black, then wiping it off again almost right away. You could also try this using other colors, such as Metallic Rust and Metallic Bronze.

PAINTING WITH A TOOTHPICK

Even though a good script brush (they have *really* long bristles) can make an incredibly fluid line, it still requires an extremely steady hand and lots of practice to achieve. We have discovered that a round toothpick is much easier to control than a script brush! You dip your toothpick into the paint and use a tight, stippling motion, as if the toothpick were the needle in a sewing machine. The purpose of using this motion is to keep the paint coverage solid and steady for the length of the line you are painting. Otherwise, the tip of the toothpick will carve a streak through the luminous paint.

PAINTING STRIPES

A dramatic, and more complex, method of color blocking is painting stripes or pin striping. Stripes are a great way to give your design a bit sophistication or playfulness. You can do this to any part of the shoe, including the heel!

An easy way to achieve stripes is using low-tack tape and masking off the lines you don't want to paint. Masking tape comes in many different, pre-cut widths as small as half inch. And, if you want really fine stripes, check out your local auto parts store for automotive detailing tape!

Remember to press the length of tape firmly with your thumb when you apply it, so no paint bleeds under the edge. (If you are worried about equal spacing, you can use small pieces of tape between your stripes as spacers. Just don't forget to remove them before you start painting!) After the paint dries, peel up the tape slowly with as much patience as you can muster because you don't want to damage those crisp lines.

SEA SPONGING

Sponge painting creates a nice dappled effect. Choose a sponge with small points and cut off a piece small enough to easily work with. Pour a very small amount of paint onto a flat palette. Spread it around so you have just a thin layer of paint.

Dab your sponge LIGHTLY in the paint, then dab it on the piece of paper (to test what kind of pattern it will make and remove any excess paint) before LIGHTLY dabbing the insole. Dab with an up-and-down motion, so you don't make streaks. You'll get the best results if you don't saturate the sponge. You want the sponge's little pointy parts to stay fairly stiff, not get all soft and wet. You can allow the original color to show through, as in the photo at left, or use multiple colors and completely cover the original color, as on the gladiator sandal at right. Allow to dry completely between coats.

STAMPING

It's a little tricky to use rubber stamps on shoes because the surface isn't firm or absorbent (unless you're stamping onto the fabric of the shoe). If you use deeply etched stamps without a lot of detail and don't mind a less-than-crisp look, try it. Try to choose stamps that will look good if they come out a little fuzzy, like the petroglyph stamps I used on Ancient Spirals, at left.

When you're stamping, you can use Lumiere or the other leather paints, but you'll have to use a lightly coated brush to apply the paint to the stamp (and wash off your stamp before the paint dries on it).Otherwise, you can use stamp pads whose ink will adhere to leather, such as StazOn by Tsukineko. When you stamp the shoe, hold something inside the shoe to create a flat, hard surface for the stamp to press against. I used a small square of tile; use your imagination and you'll find something that will work.

REVERSE STENCILING

Even if, like Margot, you can't paint things that look like things, you can put little silhouette shapes (like fleur-de-lys, martini glasses, cats, butterflies, etc.) on your shoes using a technique we call reverse stenciling. Start by finding or making stickers in the size and shapes you want on your shoes. Now paint the entire shoe the color that you

want your images to be. (On *Good Morning, Paris* on the previous page, I first painted the whole shoe Pearl White.) Let dry for at least two hours. Press your stickers onto the shoe. Then paint the shoe with one coat of paint. You could use multiple coats of paint, but it makes it harder to pull up the stickers. When the paint is *just* dry, pull up the stickers using the tip of a toothpick or hobby knife to help. Touch up the shapes with a tiny brush as needed.

Covering Areas With Fabric or Leather

You can spice up your shoes or bags by covering various distinct sections of them with fabric or leather. If the area is rectangular or flat, like on the Golders Green bag on the front of this book, all you need to do is measure, cut and glue. If the area is on a shoe or it's an irregular shape, you'll need to either use very stretchy fabric (like the black lace on Pretty in Pink at left) and rough cut the shape, letting the elasticity of the fabric make up for your inexactness, or you'll need to make a little pattern for the area.

To make a pattern, start with the LEFT shoe. Take a piece of paper and press it over the area you want to cover. Hold the paper with one hand, and with the other, use the edge of your thumbnail to press a crease into the paper along the ridges of the shoe where the distinct area begins and ends. Remove the paper, mark the crease with a dark pen and label it LEFT. Repeat the process for the RIGHT shoe. Now cut out these shapes with scissors and try to fit onto the shoe. Trim the shapes as needed. Ta-da! You have a pattern. Cut out your fabric (preferably on the bias) or leather and glue, using the Sassy Feet Glue Guide on Page 30 to choose the appropriate glue.

Metallic Leafing

Applying metallic leaf—gold, copper, silver, colored or multicolored leaf—to the parts of your shoes that don't flex or bend is quite simple, if a little messy. And it looks fabulous on a broad surface like the sides of a wedge. Metallic leafing supplies can be found in craft stores. You

will need the metallic leaf itself, brush-on adhesive, and brush-on sealant.

The first step is to brush on a thin coat of sealer (using your fan brush). When it's dry (about 30 minutes), brush on an equally thin coat of adhesive. Wait until the

adhesive is dry but tacky to the touch (30 minutes. Now cover your work surface with a large sheet of paper to catch the inevitable stray flakes of leaf. Open the bag of metallic flakes and remove a clump with tweezers. Sprinkle them over a section of the adhesive. With a wide soft brush, rub the flakes well into the now-tacky surface. Spread them around so that any loose flakes or specks get grabbed by the adhesive.

Continue working this way until all areas are covered. At this point, you'll probably notice that there are some places where the flakes didn't stick. Those are spots that got skipped when you brushed on the adhesive. Dab adhesive on those spots, wait 30 minutes and apply leafing. When all the leafing is done, brush on a final coat of sealer and let dry.

CHAPTER 5
FOR ONE-OF-A-KIND BRIDES

One of the things I love best about shoes is that they take us places, sometimes places we've never been before. And what better symbol for stepping into a new life — like a marriage — than wearing shoes that make a statement about your personal style or speak your intentions for your new life (see I Promise You on Page 50). When you paint and embellish shoes, you can make your bridal shoes as unique as you are.

Some brides ask us, "But will people *see* them?" Oh yes! They'll peep out beneath your gown as you walk down the aisle, make an appearance when you descend the steps of the church (or City Hall), and show themselves off scandalously during the infamous "garter shot," beloved of grooms and best men alike!

Adornment is never anything except a reflection of the heart.

COCO CHANEL

GALLERY: BRIDAL AND FLOWER GIRL SHOES

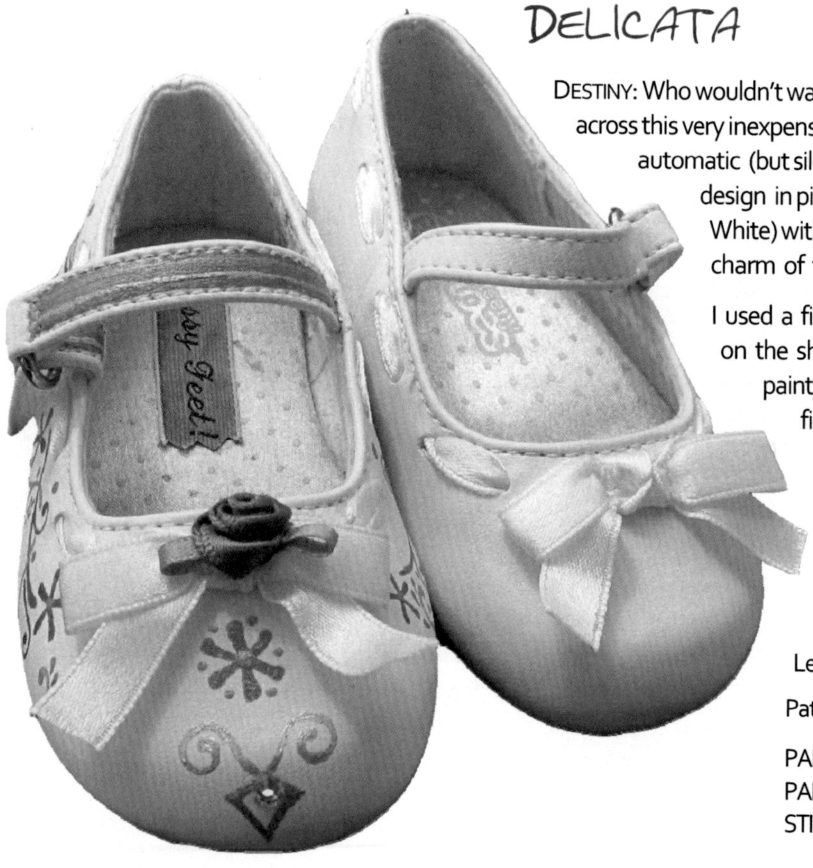

DELICATA

DESTINY: Who wouldn't want to paint baby shoes? They're so cute! When I came across this very inexpensive pair at Payless, their sheer tininess triggered an automatic (but silent) "Awww!" I thought an ornate and fluid floral design in pink (mixed from Pearlescent Magenta and Pearl White) with touches of Metallic Silver and Citrine would suit the charm of these sweet Mary Janes.

I used a fine paintbrush to create the petals of the flowers on the shoes, dipping the full length of the bristles into the paint, then pressing the side onto the shoe. The curling filigree was done with a toothpick. Two tiny roses from a craft store were stitched across the little bows that were already on the shoes. These tiny flower girls shoes have been featured in *Altered Couture* magazine.

Cost of materials:
Level of difficulty:
Patience required:

PAINTING, PAGE 18
PAINTING WITH A TOOTHPICK, PAGE 43
STITCHING ON EMBELLISHMENTS, PAGE 28

LITTLE VIOLET

MARGOT: Why should grownups have all the shoe-embellishment fun? I took a pair of classic toddler shoes with white strap and buckle and decided to paint them a glorious, luminous lavender . I mixed the color by adding a little Pearlescent Violet to Pearl White. Then I went digging through my drawers of trim and came up with a piece of organza and chenille flower trim, which I found online.

This trim (often used on pillows and purses) is mounted on an elastic band, which makes it easy to fit around the curving top line of the shoe. I chose to glue on the trim, but you could stitch it on for extra security if you think the shoes will get heavy use. These little darlings (if I do say so myself) have been featured in *Altered Couture* magazine.

Cost of materials:
Level of difficulty:
Patience required:

PAINTING, PAGE 18
GLUING ON TRIM, PAGE 30

DANCER'S DELIGHT

DESTINY: These are some of the least expensive bridal shoes I've altered. The shoes originally came from Target. They are manmade leather with a weave imprint resembling satin, but much easier to keep clean! I added embellishments from the world of scrapbooking – large and small organza flowers and silver leaf ribbon climbing up and around the ankle straps and toes, all glued on. Simple and very cute! These lightweight heels have been featured in *Altered Couture* magazine.

Cost of materials:
Level of difficulty:
Patience required:

GLUING ON TRIM, PAGE 30

CINDERELLA DREAMS

DESTINY: Some brides want shoes they can be comfortable in all the way to the end of the reception. These tucked ivory ballet flats fit the bill. I added ivory Venise lace around the throat of the shoe, and painted highlights on it with Lumiere's Metallic Gold. At the tip of each point of the lace, I hot-fixed a Swarovski crystal. Then I found an elaborate rhinestone-and-gold cloak clasp at a fabric overstock outlet and stitched one half of the fastener to the toe of each shoe. It looks like a fancy medallion and added a Renaissance touch — at an outlet price! These "dreams" have been featured in *Altered Couture* magazine.

Cost of materials: 👠👠👠👠
Level of difficulty: 👠👠👠👠
Patience required: 👠👠👠👠

GLUING ON TRIM, PAGE 30
ATTACHING CRYSTALS, PAGE 31
STITCHING ON EMBELLISHMENTS, PAGE 28

Go confidently in the direction of your dreams. Live the life you imagine.

HENRY DAVID THOREAU

IVORY SWIRLS

MARGOT: This was one of those shoe designs born from the discovery of a fabulous trim. I found this swirling, spiral-wrapped passementerie at a lace specialty store called Lacis in Berkeley, Calif. It wasn't cheap, but I immediately snapped up a couple yards in ivory and black (see *Ruffles at Midnight* on Page 25). The generous area provided by this high wedge was the perfect backdrop for showing off this trim. Once I had glued it down, I stitched pearls onto it. The final touch was gluing a strand of freshwater pearls down the delicately curving seam line of the wedge.

Cost of materials: 👠👠👠👠
Level of difficulty: 👠👠👠👠
Patience required: 👠👠👠👠

GLUING ON TRIM, PAGE 30
STITCHING ON EMBELLISHMENTS, PAGE 28

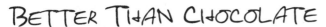

BETTER THAN CHOCOLATE

DESTINY: This little bootie is the hands-down favorite when we take our collection of bridal shoes to Wedding Fairs. I used color blocking with Lumiere's Metallic Rust paint on the larger areas and a darker, flatter color of brown (from a line called Neopaque by Jacquard) for painting the little pointed edges. A 3"-wide brownish-purple, gold-edged organza ribbon is tied in a big poufy bow, replacing the original plain laces. This is another great example of simple, easy-to-do changes that make a huge impact. These booties have been featured in *Altered Couture* magazine.

Cost of materials: 🥿🥿🥿🥿

Level of difficulty: 🥿🥿🥿🥿

Patience required: 🥿🥿🥿🥿

PAINTING, PAGE 18
COLOR BLOCKING, PAGE 20
SASSIFYING YOUR SHOELACES, PAGE 32

ELOPE WITH ME

DESTINY: A lot goes on during a bride's big day — most of which involves being on her feet. I adapted a pair of Skechers z-Strap sneakers for brides who want comfortable shoes to slip into after the ceremony. Leaving the bulk of the sneakers white, I dyed a small piece of stretch lace in light pink, then inset it into the recessed area of the toe design. I also hand-dyed a length of pearly trim to glue onto the z-Strap — this worked out very nicely as the pearls (plastic) stayed white, but the surrounding cord turned pink. I also hand-dyed some ruffled cotton lace to use as piping around the throat of the shoe. A silver charm in the shape of an iris dangles playfully from the back seam. Sweet, bridal — and blessedly comfortable!

Cost of materials: 🥿🥿🥿🥿

Level of difficulty: 🥿🥿🥿🥿

Patience required: 🥿🥿🥿🥿

ATTACHING PIPING, PAGE 31
GLUING ON TRIM, PAGE 30
STITCHING ON EMBELLISHMENTS, PAGE 28
COVERING AREAS WITH FABRIC OR LEATHER, PAGE 45

LACE CURTAINS

DESTINY: Who doesn't love a Burnt Orange Boot?! Of course, it *did* take three coats over the white leather to achieve a nice even color. Surprisingly, white is a lot more stubborn than black to paint over! This wouldn't have mattered if I'd been painting at home, but I mistakenly took this project to a women's craft fair to use as the subject of a painting demonstration. Anyone who saw the boot during coats #1 and #2 were not that impressed! By coat #3, though, we were garnering all sorts of praise.

Once I finally got the boot a soft gleaming orange, I used a toothpick and Lumiere's Pearl White to create a delicate filigree design on the ankle and toe area. Last of all, I encircled the top of the boot with deeply fringed, snowy white Venise lace dotted with flatback hotfix "pearls" to compliment the handpainted design.

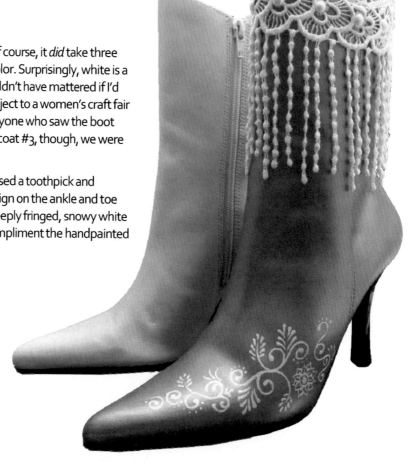

Cost of materials:
Level of difficulty:
Patience required:

PAINTING, PAGE 18
PAINTING WITH A TOOTHPICK, PAGE 43
GLUING ON TRIM, PAGE 30

I PROMISE YOU

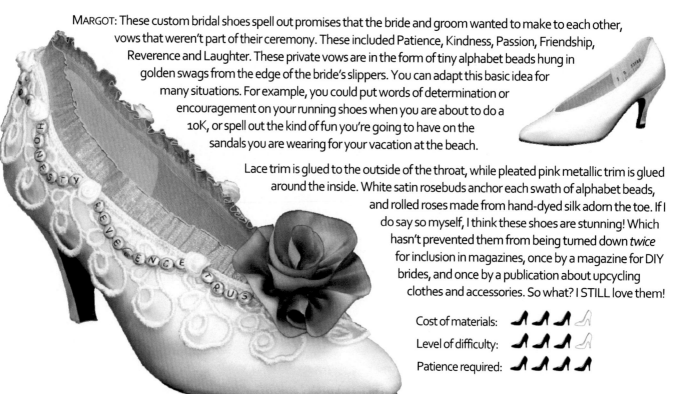

MARGOT: These custom bridal shoes spell out promises that the bride and groom wanted to make to each other, vows that weren't part of their ceremony. These included Patience, Kindness, Passion, Friendship, Reverence and Laughter. These private vows are in the form of tiny alphabet beads hung in golden swags from the edge of the bride's slippers. You can adapt this basic idea for many situations. For example, you could put words of determination or encouragement on your running shoes when you are about to do a 10K, or spell out the kind of fun you're going to have on the sandals you are wearing for your vacation at the beach.

Lace trim is glued to the outside of the throat, while pleated pink metallic trim is glued around the inside. White satin rosebuds anchor each swath of alphabet beads, and rolled roses made from hand-dyed silk adorn the toe. If I do say so myself, I think these shoes are stunning! Which hasn't prevented them from being turned down *twice* for inclusion in magazines, once by a magazine for DIY brides, and once by a publication about upcycling clothes and accessories. So what? I STILL love them!

Cost of materials:
Level of difficulty:
Patience required:

ATTACHING PIPING, PAGE 31 — GLUING ON TRIM, PAGE 30 — STITCHING ON EMBELLISHMENTS, PAGE 28

Fashions fade, but style is eternal.

COCO CHANEL

CHAPTER 6
UPCYCLING BAGS AND HANDBAGS

Okay, we admit it: It took us an embarrassingly long time to realize that whatever we could do to shoes, we could do to purses. What's more, when we turned our attention to these much-loved companions of our lives, we discovered we could actually do more, like change handles to shoulder straps or attach king-sized embellishments that wouldn't work on shoes. And what a forum for the imagination! Upcycling handbags is SERIOUS fun!

GALLERY: BAGS AND HANDBAGS

FULL MOON

MARGOT: After a friend's very stylish mother passed away in her mid-nineties, I inherited many of her handbags, all lovingly

cared for over the decades. This one started out dark red and my first step was to paint it Neopaque Black. Next I chose strong Lumiere colors that would contrast with the black background, were similar in value, and would look yummy together. I picked Pearlescent Blue, Pearlescent Violet, Metallic Olive Green, Metallic Bronze and Metallic Russet.

I used the flat side of a wedge-shaped cosmetic sponge to dab the colors on with a light touch, leaving some of the black background showing. When I got done, I had paint leftover on my palette, so I grabbed a black leather wallet I'd picked up from one of our local thrift stores, prepped it with rubbing alcohol, and went to work with a fresh cosmetic wedge, daubing it front and back.

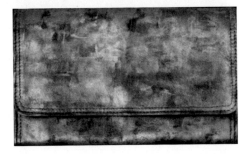

P.S. I made the embellishment from a large Asian coin daubed with Lumiere Metallic Olive Green topped with a dichroic glass square and an imitation ivory button carved to look like a moon/face. Technically, Lumiere is not formulated to adhere to metal, but I find that if the metal surface is not going to be subjected to abrasion, the paint stays on just fine.

Cost of materials: 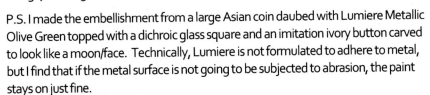 PAINTING, PAGE 18
COSMETIC SPONGING, PAGE 58
STITCHING ON EMBELLISHMENTS, PAGE 28

Level of difficulty:

Patience required: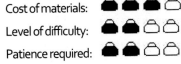

TYGER, TYGER

DESTINY: The existing lines on a
bag or shoe will often help steer
your design. On this clutch I chose to
paint the two diagonal panels Sunset
Gold, which is a complementary color to
the purple of the original bag. Then I hand
painted a tiger-stripe design diagonally in the
opposite direction to bump up the visual interest. If you can't paint "things that look like things" — as Margot puts it, when describing her
own painting ability — you can always use a stencil or do a design transfer (see Page 21) onto the purse. Last of all, I glued a fiery Paula
Radke dichroic lozenge over the magnetic clasp to really make the design POP!

Cost of materials:
Level of difficulty:
Patience required:

PAINTING, PAGE 18
TRANSFERRING DESIGNS, PAGE 21
GLUING ON EMBELLISHMENTS, PAGE 29

OFF THE STREETS

DESTINY: Okay, I admit it: This design is me showing off. I love graffiti art and have
always wanted to incorporate it into one of my handbag designs. I started upcycling
this bag by dyeing the gray suede panels on the front dark purple. Then I painted all
the gray leather with Neopaque Black and sealed it.
Once it was *thoroughly* dry, I pressed down strips of
masking tape to create a city skyline on the flap. I
lightly daubed Lumiere's Grape paint just above the
buildings. Next I used Sparkling Silver and Royal Purple
Glitter It glaze to fill in the starry night sky. You'll notice
that I did not paint the whole background of the sky in
Grape. This is because I wanted the glitter to allow the
black of the "sky" show through.

On the reverse side, this bag had a large flat surface
that just screamed "TAG ME!!!" I sketched a graffiti-
style design and filled it in with a multitude of cool
blues and purples with Neopaque Black edges. Like
most graffiti artists, as I painted I got a little carried
away and the design spread to the front of the bag. I
loved the results — it was like a hint of the fabulous
secret on the other side.

Cost of materials:
Level of difficulty:
Patience required:

DYEING SUEDE, PAGE 21
PAINTING, PAGE 18
GLITTERING, PAGE 21

GOLDERS GREEN

MARGOT: Curiosity may have killed the cat, but it is the very lifeblood of an artisan. I created this purse because the label on Lumiere says it works on straw — and I wanted to see if it really did. Well, it worked like a dream and there was no need to prep the surface. I chose Lumiere's Citrine and Sunset Gold, painting them on with alternating swipes of the brush. Next I cut off the strap and covered its stub with a fabric-and-trim collage. This consisted of three Kaffe Fassett cotton prints and a piece of metallic-looking trim from an outlet store. I stitched the three fabric strips together, then glued them and the trim onto the straw. The last step was to attach a new shoulder strap. I used decorative cord from a home dec store. Since enough is rarely enough for me, I added a coordinating jumbo tassel from the same home dec department.

Cost of materials:
Level of difficulty:
Patience required:

PAINTING, PAGE 18
GLUING ON TRIM, PAGE 30
CHANGING HANDLES OR SHOULDER STRAPS, PAGE 58

SEA STAR

MARGOT: This purse began as a cattle-country design featuring natural-grain leather and a star of Texas in white hair-on cowhide. I decided to give it a trip to California. I started my redesign at a seashell shop, where I went around surreptitiously testing various shells for durability — I didn't want to attach anything fragile to the bag. The winner was a pillow sea star. I also found a hank of black fishing net, too, though I had no idea what I'd do with it. I just... liked it!

I glued a button back to the sea star and while waiting for it to dry overnight, I got out my paints. I chose Pearlescent Blue for the body of the purse and Neopaque Black for the straps. I also tinted the hair on the white cow-hair star blue with Jacquard's Piñata Colors ink. I stitched the sea star over the Western star and sat back, please with myself. For a while. Then I realized I hadn't done enough.

I got out the fishing net and started playing with it. Before I was through, I had stitched it around the top of the bag, covered the raw edge with flat black cord, drawn it up on one, side and tied it with ribbon like a beach bunny's ponytail. Done? Nope. Last of all, I went back to the seashell shop and bought several chunks of sea glass. I glued them onto silver bails and hung them in the "tail" of the fish net. Then I stopped and went for a walk — on the beach, of course.

PAINTING, PAGE 18
STITCHING ON EMBELLISHMENTS, PAGE 28
GLUING ON EMBELLISHMENTS, PAGE 29

Cost of materials:
Level of difficulty:
Patience required:

PIRATE GIRL

DESTINY AND MARGOT: In the late 1990s, a fashion epidemic of bustier purses hit the marketplace full force. For months, lacy, patent leather and fabric handbags hung from retailer shelves like tiny corsets on display. Then, as quickly as the fad erupted, it petered out again. We've developed a new look for these bags, which you can usually find on ebay, sometimes in rather violent colors.

We started by painting the whole purse Neopaque Black. Then we went to work turning this tarty bustier into a pirate wench's bodice. We used red stretch lace to cover the cups, then glued a narrow strip of flat faux-leather cord around the edges. For a swashbuckling centerpiece, we wanted to use an iron-on rhinestone motif, but in our experience, iron-on and hot-fix glues aren't permanent on leather or manmade leather. We realized, though, that we could iron this motif onto black fabric, then trim the edges and glue the fabric to the bag. Above the skull, we stitched a silver pirate's cutlass.

Now we turned to the little handles. Too girly for a pirate. We cut them off as close to the bag as possible, then touched up the raw edges with more black paint. We replaced the handles with a 24" choke-chain collar for dogs. Were we done? No way! Gotta go one — or two or three — steps further. We strung a couple strands of skull beads, tied them onto one end of the chain, and added a red tassel.

Hands down, this purse gets the most attention when we are teaching classes and doing shows!

Cost of materials: 🌑🌑⚪⚪
Level of difficulty: 🌑🌑🌑⚪
Patience required: 🌑🌑🌑⚪

PAINTING, PAGE 18
COVERING AREAS WITH FABRIC OR LEATHER, PAGE 45
 GLUING ON TRIM, PAGE 30
ATTACHING CRYSTALS, PAGE 31
STITCHING ON EMBELLISHMENTS , PAGE 28

Life's pretty good, and why wouldn't it be? I'm a pirate, after all.
JOHNNY DEPP

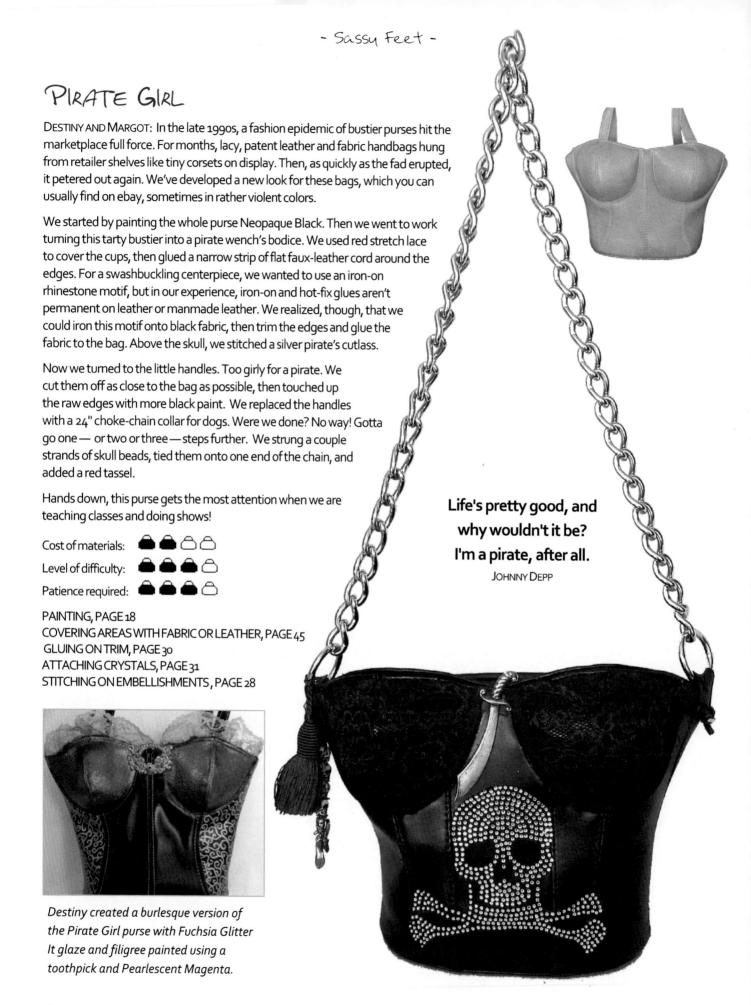

Destiny created a burlesque version of the Pirate Girl purse with Fuchsia Glitter It glaze and filigree painted using a toothpick and Pearlescent Magenta.

STEAMPUNK TIME

MARGOT: This little purse is just 6 ½" wide by 5 ½" high so I'm not sure why I decide to do so many different painting and embellishing techniques on it. Maybe I'm just contrary…. Or maybe it was the fact that it already had different types of embossing, which I thought would look cool rubbed, painted and/or glittered. I started with the left-hand panel of embossing, brushing on Citrine paint and rubbing most of it off so the embossing would show up. Then I highlighted the embossing with black Neopaque paint, Citrine (full-strength), and Glitter It glaze in Peridot. I did the same thing on the upper right panel of embossing, this time using Pearlescent White for the undercoat.

Next I rummaged through my stash and came up with some treasures. The large central panel got painted and rubbed, then I glued down a black web-like ribbon. I covered the lower panel with green stretch lace. The top left panel has three rows of big black satin cord, striped ribbon, a bar of Peridot Glitter It glaze, and some tiny black-loop trim. Final touches were to attach a vintage watch face, replace the strap with heavy gunmetal curb chain, and add a large black rayon tassel.

Cost of materials: ●●○○○

Level of difficulty: ●●●○

Patience required: ●●●○

PAINTING, PAGE 18
GLITTERING, PAGE 21
GLUING ON TRIM, PAGE 30
COVERING AREAS WITH FABRIC OR LEATHER, PAGE 45
STITCHING ON EMBELLISHMENTS, PAGE 28
CHANGING HANDLES OR SHOULDER STRAPS, PAGE 58

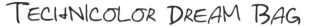

TECHNICOLOR DREAM BAG

MARGOT: Have you ever bought something you thought was really great, used it once or twice, and left it to sit in your closet for four years? That's what I did with this bag until one day I hauled it out and gave it a makeover. I used the cosmetic-sponging technique where you dab and daub on the color. For this bag, I chose Pearlescent Violet, Metallic Bronze, Super Copper, Metallic Russet, and Metallic Olive.

Next I painted the leather trim and piping and pocket flap in solid colors, using masking tape to cover the sponged areas. Then I went back to my stash to find embellishments for the flap. I came across some leather beads I'd found one day at a bead show. (Who knew there was such a thing?) I stitched them onto the flap and hoisted the bag on my shoulder. It's my everyday bag now, and it's happy to have come out of the closet.

Cost of materials:
Level of difficulty:
Patience required:

PAINTING, PAGE 18
COSMETIC SPONGING, PAGE 58
STITCHING ON EMBELLISHMENTS, PAGE 28

VINTAGE STEAMPUNK

MARGOT: When I decided to upcycle this paint-damaged purse, I determined to deck it out with my favorite embellishments — metal mesh roses, vintage watch faces, rusty-looking gears, and chain maille! I painted the purse with Lumiere's Halo Pink Gold, then antiqued it using Neopaque Black paint. I also decided to paint the handles of the purse black. Then Destiny and my favorite mixed-media artist, Erin Perry of Altered by the Sea, helped me figure out the best placement for my embellishments. We "auditioned" them using earthquake/poster/museum putty, then took a photo of the final arrangement. This was necessary because I had to dismantle the design to glue some of the pieces together before stitching them onto the purse. Once they were all in place, we tweaked the design one last time by deciding to smudge the big red roses with a little black Staz-On stamp pad ink (it works on metal), and smudge some of the chain maille with dark red Staz-On.

Cost of materials:
Level of difficulty:
Patience required:

PAINTING, PAGE 18
STITCHING ON EMBELLISHMENTS, PAGE 28
STITCHING ON CHAIN, PAGE 29

CHERRY BLOSSOM TOTE

MARGOT: The challenge with painting this tote was twofold. First was its sheer size — it was so tall that at first I couldn't figure out how to make it look interesting. Second, I really, really wanted to have a spray of cherry blossoms arching across the front, but I can't paint things that look like things. Destiny suggested I do color blocking for the background to break up the expanse of black (the color I'd painted the whole tote). She helped me choose the size and placement of color blocks and advised on the colors. I painted in the blocks, doing a little repainting as my eye dictated. I also painted the straps Metallic Olive. Then I tackled the issue of the cherry blossoms. I realized that I could use a stencil to trace a spray cherry blossoms before painting them in by hand. I found a stencil that would fit the tote, taped it in place with masking tape and traced the design using a white paint pen (see inset above). The rest was like paint-by-number. Destiny advised me mixing the right shade for the branches and highlighting the centers of the blossoms with Sunset Gold. I finished off the tote with an embellishment I'd made and a chiffon scarf purchased years ago on my honeymoon at a market stall in Paris. Who says totes can't be feminine?

Cost of materials: ■■□□□
Level of difficulty: ■■□□□
Patience required: ■■□□□

PAINTING, PAGE 18
STENCILING, PAGE 20
STITCHING ON EMBELLISHMENTS, PAGE 28

MARGARET MEAD LAPTOP/CARRY-ON BAG

DESTINY: Welcome to Typography Land! Designs don't have to just be images. I am a quote junky: great lines or inspiring words from movies, books, articles, proverbs, you name it. Margot and I both love this quote from anthropologist Margaret Mead, and I was more than happy to paint this manmade leather laptop/carryon bag for her as a birthday present. I sketched out the words first using white chalk. It took several tries to get everything to fit. When I didn't like something I'd chalked in, I could use a paper towel (and a little water) to wipe the bag without ruining the surface.

When the design was finalized, I chose colors I like and repeated them in order: Pewter, Citrine, Metallic Russet, Sunset Gold, and Pearlescent Blue. As you can see, I imitated different typefaces and decorated some of the letters with lines, spatters and other details to increase the interest. I painted everything using a medium round brush.

Cost of materials: ■■□□□
Level of difficulty: ■■■□□
Patience required: ■■■□□

PAINTING, PAGE 18

ADDITIONAL TECHNIQUES USED IN THIS CHAPTER

COSMETIC SPONGING

This technique calls for using a wedge-shaped cosmetic sponge to dab several colors of paint over a contrasting background. You dab each color on sparsely, one at a time, and let each color dry before dabbing on the next. Don't pick up a big blob of each color -- just a bit. Simply use the sponge to mix the colors on the leather itself. Also, don't worry about the paint drying before applying more.

When you sponge, dab the sponge. Don't drag or mush it around or you'll end up with mud instead of nice distinct colors. In the bag above, I used the flat bottom of the sponge and dabbed the paint on horizontally, then at the very end I did some vertical dabs (thanks to the recommendation of my friend Leanne) with the edge of the sponge to create more visual interest.

One of the most fun thing about this method is choosing your colors. Nearly all the Lumiere colors — there are 25 — look great together, so you're pretty much assured of good results. For the Full Moon bag, I chose strong colors that would contrast with the black background and were similar in value. I picked Lumiere Pearlescent Blue, Pearlescent Violet, Metallic Olive Green, Metallic Bronze and Metallic Russet. At left is a close-up of the paint pattern.

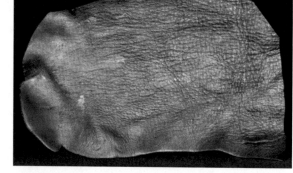

If you want, you can cover the entire background, sponge more densely and get a very different result. At right is a detailed shot of this technique using Lumiere Pearl Magenta, Crimson, Burgundy, Halo Violet Gold, Grape and Metallic Bronze. These are dark and light shades of red, purple and bronze. I squeezed a little puddle of each onto a palette, then used a wedge-shaped cosmetic sponge to daub small amounts of the colors onto a sample scrap of leather. Here's what the sample looked like.

CHANGING HANDBAG HANDLES OR SHOULDER STRAPS

One of the fun things to do when you are upcycling a handbag is to change its handles or shoulder strap. You can even change from one to the other. On Golders Green, at right, Margot replaced the narrow manmade-leather strap with a luxurious length of upholstery cord. On Pirate Girl, on the next page, we replaced the short and not-very-useful little handles with a heavy weight shoulder strap of chain — actually a dog's choke-chain collar! It goes great with the pirate motif!

Let's take them one at a time. To replace a shoulder strap, either carefully detach it or just cut it off. On Golders Green, the shoulder strap had a little leather placket (just visible on the before photo) helping secure it to the outside of the bag. Margot coped with that by covering the area with fabric, which was part of her plan anyway. This bag used about 34" of 3/8" multicolor upholstery cording.

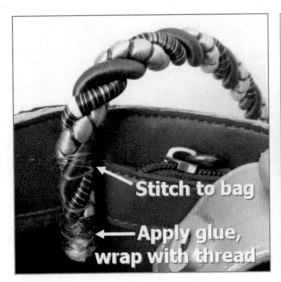

Before cutting it to the right length, apply glue inside where you will cut, squeezing it between the plies, and wrap with upholstery thread. (See enlargement at right.) Now cut a clean end of the cord. Repeat for the other end. Position the cord inside the bag and stitch in place using FireLine or DandyLine beading thread. Often, you will be able to stitch down the cording without having to push the needle all the way to the outside of the bag. If you do have to do that, you can either make sure the stitches on the outside are small and discreet, or, as Margot did, you can cover the stitches with trim or embellishments.

The same goes when replacing handbag handles. Detach or cut them off. Paint the raw edges of your cut handles when you paint the bag. Or, leave a 2" to 2½" stub at the point where you cut each handle and use that to anchor your new strap or handles. (You can stitch the new strap directly to the stub or, better yet, use a chain as your strap and loop the stub through it.) Then fold the stub in two and stitch it to itself. You can do this on the inside or outside of the bag.

The stub turns into a little tab holding your new strap in place, as shown on Steampunk Time, at right. If you use this alternative, don't try to glue the stubs closed, stitch them. Handbags get too much stress to trust their straps or handles to mere glue.)

We did a variation of this on Pirate Girl, below. We removed the original handles, then used fairly strong scrap leather to cut two tabs that we could use to anchor our new shoulder strap. Once we had wrapped these leather tabs around the ring at each end of the chain, we stitched the tabs onto the purse.

The qualities I find sexy in a person include intelligence, humor, and really good shoes.

STING

CHAPTER 7

JUST SHOWING OFF

Sometimes we try outrageously complicated techniques just to see if they'll work. (Not all of them do!) Other times, we are asked to pull out all the stops and create shoes for a charity auction or to show at a high-end wearable art exhibit. The shoes in this chapter go beyond our ability to explain all the techniques and steps it took to create them — but we thought you'd get a kick (pun intended) out of seeing them nonetheless.

GALLERY: OUR OVER-THE-TOP SHOES

22K WEDGES

MARGOT: These wooden wedges with their '70s embroidery cried out for an extreme update. They were also the perfect artist's canvas for some special treatment: variegated gold leafing. Applying metallic leaf is quite simple, if a little messy. And it looks fabulous on a broad surface like the sides of a wedge.

I altered this pair of sandals in several stages. First I removed the straps and painted them black (they were a very dark brown to start with). Then I painted a wide black margin all the way around the top edge of the wedge, using masking tape to create a straight line. Next I applied variegated gold leaf to the wedge. (You'll find instructions at the end of Chapter 4.) The last step was to cover the old embroidered toe area with a dark green jacquard shot through with metallic threads. I finished it off by tying on a scrap of gold lace. These wedges have been featured in *Altered Couture* magazine.

THE GOLD STANDARD

MARGOT: This is me, copying a trademark Ferragamo pump. Salvatore Ferragamo was just out of his teens, the immigrant son of an Italian peasant, when his handmade shoes took Hollywood by storm in the 1920s. Glamour was his trademark — he once created a pair of 18-karat gold sandals — and his clients ranged from Greta Garbo, Katherine Hepburn, and Lauren Bacall to Sophia Loren, Marilyn Monroe, and Audrey Hepburn. This design, reissued in 2006 to celebrate Ferragamo's eightieth anniversary, is one of just six red-carpet designs chosen for the Ferragamo Glam Collection. Featured in *Vogue*, *InStyle*, and *Elle* magazines, it cost over $700.

My Ferragamo look-alike uses Metallic Gold paint and about nine yards of inexpensive gold chain from a craft store to recreate the master's timeless look of luxury. The curtain of chain dangling was no fun to attach, but once I got it done (glue, not stitching is the key), I loved the results. I finished off the shoe by gluing more chain down the heel and back of the shoe (places where the shoe wouldn't bend and pop the chain off). Cost? Maybe $15. The Look? Priceless.

IN YOUR FACE

Margot: Sometimes you just want to do what you want to do, and you don't much care if other people think you're strange or wrong or bad. These boots caught me in a moment like this. I decided to throw caution to the winds and use whatever embellishments struck my fancy and figure out how to attach them later. After some stitching, drilling holes, gluing, attaching loops and other elaborate tactics, I managed to securely attach all of the following: Antique garters, scrabble tiles, palm tree appliqués, watch faces, dragon charms, bat stampings, broken zippers, doll-clothes zippers, old keys, escutcheons, snap tape (wrong side up), nailheads (put in backwards so only their little teeth show), sash chain, and cut-metal signs. You could call this boot my *tour de force* of attaching embellishments — even though no one has ever wanted to put it in a wearable art show or publish it in a magazine.

Can't think why not.

Urban Valentine

DESTINY AND MARGOT: A pair of brown lace-up boots of manmade leather is transformed into sexy black boots, thanks to an application of Neopaque Black and the elimination of ugly brown cotton shoelaces.

Actually, that was just the beginning. With these boots, we were aiming for over the top — and we definitely got there. We covered the heel and counter of the boot with Really Red Glitter It glaze. The long tongue of the boot was overlaid with lovely red lace, and black-on-black brocade was glued over the eyelets where the laces originally went.

Then we got out the chain maille! We fashioned an asymmetrical curtain of fine-gauge stainless steel maille and affixed it to the top edge of the boot. (This sounds *way* simpler than it was....) We bound that top edge in fine-grain perforated black leather to cushion the wearer from the metal. From the point of the chain maille, we dangled a red-lace-embellished black tassel and a Murano glass heart swinging from black bead chain. A larger gauge of chain maille and a cast sterling silver rose were used to add sass to the toe of the boot.

We are proud to say that these boots were chosen for the acclaimed Wearable Expressions exhibit in Los Angeles and later appeared in *Altered Couture* magazine.

Bourbon Street Beauties

DESTINY AND MARGOT: We designed these wonderfully over-the-top boots when we were asked to create something for a shoe-themed charity fundraiser scheduled for Mardi Gras. The event was called "Walk on the Wild Side." If that wasn't an invitation to let 'er rip, we don't know what is.

We decided to start with a pair of Victorian style booties, giving them a hint of brothel naughtiness and a lot of party attitude, but keeping them totally wearable. We started by color blocking them with two shades of Glitter It glaze (Antique Gold and Copper), then painted the heel with Lumiere's Grape. The tongue of the boot and the buttons were painted Neopaque Black. For extra sparkle, we glued amethyst-colored Swarovski crystals onto all the buttons.

Having the basic design done, we dove into our stash to find exciting, quirky, colorful and outrageous trims and accents to add some ZING! We pulled out orange guinea-feather pads, some perforated purple suede and two black beaded appliqués. These we combined into a pair of embellishments. Then we found some gold-embroidered appliqués, which we glued across the toes of the boots. Destiny touched up their lower edges with Grape Lumiere.

Then—WHAT? THERE'S MORE? Yes. When you are altering or upcycling shoes for a really special occasion or when you want them to truly be wearable art, don't stop! Always consider whether you could add something else that will really make the design POP! We added three touches. First, Destiny painted little black zebra stripes on the heel, with gold edges, to echo those on the appliqués. Next, we glued ruffled nylon net around the top edge of the bootie. And finally, we laced up the buttons with very narrow black double-faced satin ribbon.

At this point, we conceded that we were done. Even with our fertile imaginations (and huge stash) we could think of nothing else that our Bourbon Street Beauties needed! This is my very favorite kind of project, one we do together, where our different skills, gifts and tastes find a way to weave themselves into something entirely new and unexpected — our version of *laissez les bons temps rouler*!

Note: For more details on how we created these boots, read our Feb. 25, 2011 post, "Bourbon Street Beauties," on our blog, http://glittersweatshop.typepad.com.

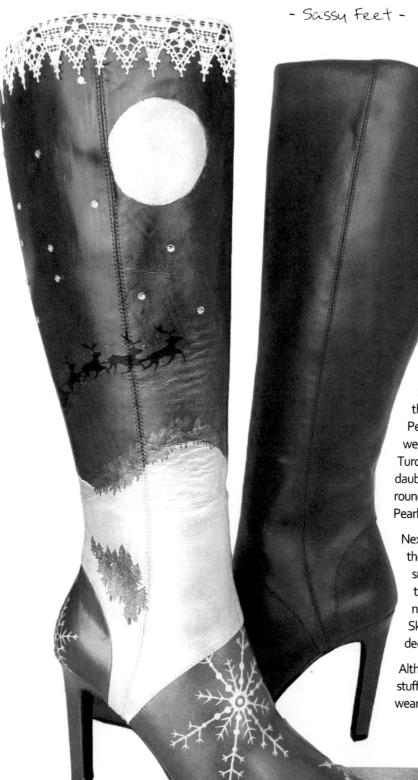

TWAS THE NIGHT BEFORE CHRISTMAS

DESTINY AND MARGOT: As a fun holiday project, we created our own Christmas stocking – out of a high heel boot! We found a boot with a nice curving shape and some lines that would lend themselves to color blocking. Destiny came up with the idea for painting a "Night Before Christmas" scene and went to work.

Starting at the top, she applied Neopaque Black, then transitioned to Lumiere's Indigo, then Pearlescent Blue. The full moon and the snowy hills were painted with Pearl White and Pearlescent Turquoise. The green of the pine trees was created by daubing on Metallic Olive Green and Citrine using a small round-pointed brush. The foot of the boot was painted Pearlescent Blue.

Next she went to work with her trusty toothpick to paint the details like Santa's sleigh and the large snowflakes. Margot added snowfall-like lace around the top and glued flatback Swarovski crystals to the night sky. Destiny dabbed a faint dusting of Midnight Sky Glitter It glaze behind Santa and his sleigh and we declared ourselves done.

Although these were designed for filling with stocking-stuffers, like all the shoes we create they are 100% wearable.

These boots were featured in the Projects section of Jacquard's website, www.jacquardproducts.com: The exact URL, as of this writing, is http://jacquardproducts.com/projects/proj0064/ .

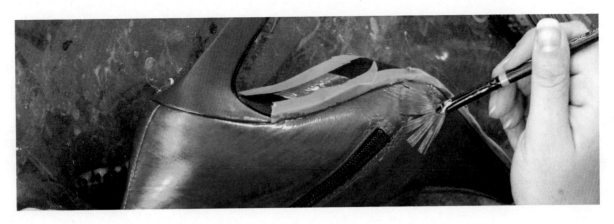

I don't look back and neither should you. Be fearless and always put your best foot forward.

MANOLO BLAHNIK

CHAPTER 8

Now It's Your Turn

Why should we have all the fun? Get yourself some paints and other supplies. Dig out an old pair of shoes or a handbag from the depths of your closet. Go shopping (we know you hate that…) for embellishments. Get your girlfriends together — and have a blast!

If you have questions or run into problems, email Margot at margot@sassyfeet.com. One of us will personally answer your email. We really, really want you to enjoy the process as well as the results of painting and embellishing shoes and handbags!

Tips on Creating Your Own Designs

When you're working on your own shoes and bags, think about it this way. If you think you're going too far, SO WHAT? Have fun with it. Shoes have to be blisteringly bold because they are waaaaaay down there, on your feet. Handbags yearn to make a personal statement. Use both of them as a canvas to SHOWCASE your individual style.

Mostly, know when NOT to stop! Our very best designs have come about because we didn't stop when we had done everything we planned to do. We kept looking at what we'd created, thinking about what else we might add. Two good examples of this are the little zebra-like stripes on the heels of Bourbon Street Beauties (Page 63) and the tiny Bali beads and freshwater pearls on Gypsy Summer (Page 11).

If you are wondering where to begin creating a design for doing your shoes or bags, here are the two main starting points we use.

Start With Something You Love

When you first start shopping for paints and embellishments to use on your shoes, you are quite likely to fall in love with something you find. For Margot, it was the luscious colors of Lumiere paint. For Destiny, it was always doing for something different, unusual, and edgy. For you it may be a 2" wide ribbon with big red beets embroidered on it. (Yes, there is such a thing: See Laura Foster Nicholson's site, www.lfntextiles.com.) The bottom line is, build your design around something you just LOVE, whether it's a color, a combination of colors, a style, an embellishment, or an eclectic assortment of embellishments.

If you want to play around with colors, it helps to make yourself a set of paint chips (little rectangles, about 3" by 1 ½") using watercolor paper or leather scraps. Try them out on your shoes or bag by attaching them with masking tape. Don't worry about whether the colors you find yourself attracted to will go with lots of things in your wardrobe. Creating upcycled shoes is so inexpensive, you can afford to have an outrageous pair or two (or three or four). Ditto handbags. That's part of the fun of DIY!

When you are designing a shoe or bag around an embellishment you love, use adhesive/poster/museum putty or drafting tape to try out how your embellishment will look on different parts of your shoe. (Caution: If your shoe is made of fabric, use masking tape instead. Putty can be hard to get off fabric.) Press the embellishment in place, then step back and really look.

Will the placement you are choosing put undue stress on the embellishment? For example, the inner face of your shoe (the "big-toe side") gets much more wear than the outer face because it tends to scuff against your other shoe. And, as we all know, the heel of the shoe gets a lot of wear and tear when we drive.

Also ask yourself if there is any other place on your shoe where the embellishment might have greater impact. Try out unexpected, even unlikely places. If you want to put a big flower on your ballet flats, for example, you could put it on the side rather than center it on the toe. If it won't interfere with walking or rub against your foot, the embellishment could even project above the throat of the shoe. Margot used both these strategies on Fan Dance (Page 33).

Go back through the Gallery sections of each chapter and look for the design choices we made, as opposed to simply viewing the finished design. Then come up with wonderful new design choices of your own! (And send us before-and-after photos to put on our blog, http://glittersweatshop.typepad.com.)

START WITH A MISCHIEVOUS GLEAM IN YOUR EYE

This is our favorite method of shoe design. Maybe it's because we're both the kind of people who respond to a "Wet Paint" sign by poking their fingers onto the paint to see if it really is wet. Maybe it's because we've read too many *Eloise* books. Whatever the reason, we've found that our natural mischievousness is a wonderful ally when designing shoes and bags.

Here are some of the mischievous combinations of materials you'll find on shoes and purses in this book.

- Crystals and black lace on a sport shoe (Pretty in Pink, Page 40)
- Iridescent dichroic glass and sheer chiffon on an utilitarian tote bag (Cherry Blossom Tote, Page 57)
- Marabou and rhinestones on a work boot (Working Girl, Page 24)
- A cameo hanging from the cuff of a bootie (Fringe Benefits, Page 35)
- Traditional tattoo art on a high-fashion platform heel (A Vintage Affair, Page 17)

Now it's your turn. See what the mischievous, playful spirit inside you can dream up — then make what you dream. Any challenges, ask us for advice!

TIPS ON BUYING EMBELLISHMENTS

The embellishments and trim you buy need to be sturdy enough to survive on feet that drive, walk on concrete, and occasionally kick things (intentionally or not). They can be stain- and waterproofed, so don't worry about that, but do worry about using things that are easily breakable.

Is the embellishment large enough to be seen from a distance? Is it so big it will be a nuisance? Is it too small to be appreciated? Small charms that would look great on a bracelet or earrings, for example, will be lost on the front of a shoe or bag unless they are used in clusters. (If you find something tiny that you simply have to use, you can hang it from the back of your shoe.) The same goes for narrow embroidered ribbon. Unless you want those little red roses to add just a dash of color, buy wider ribbon so the roses will look like roses.

When it comes to beads, gems, silver, and gold, don't spend your money on the real thing. Cheap glass beads (instead of art glass), imitation gemstones, and silver- and gold-plated charms and chains will look just fine. The same is true for silk ribbon. I like to use it because I'm a fabric snob, but polyester ribbon can be beautiful too and it's much cheaper. The only exception to this rule is crystals: Buy genuine Swarovski crystals. Nothing else sparkles half as brightly.

If you are doing shoes, remember to buy two of everything! And if the design of the embellishment (be it a brooch, stamping, or bracelet link) is clearly oriented toward the left or right, think about how that will look. I found a treasure trove of vintage-looking brass and silver-plate angel wings in an antique store one day and bought five or six different styles only to get home and discover they were all right wings! (No pun intended.)

Last of all, keep track of where you bought each kind of trim or embellishment. I guarantee that at some point you'll want or need more of it!

Remember to buy two of everything! You'll need one for each shoe. If the design of the embellishment (be it brooch, stamping, or bracelet link) is clearly oriented toward the left or right, think about how that will look. I found a treasure trove of vintage-looking brass and silver-plate angel wings in an antique store one day and bought five or six different

20 KINDS OF STORES/SITES AND THE EMBELLISHMENTS YOU CAN FIND

Antique stores/sites	Vintage buttons, chains, bracelets, earrings, shoe clips, charms, old coins.
Beading stores/sites	Cord, seed beads, bugle beads, glass beads, flatback crystals, alphabet beads, imitation gemstones, charms, pendants, metal chains, crystal chains, bracelets, earrings.
Belly-dance websites	Large chains, rhinestone chains (at good prices), and coins with loops for hanging.
Button websites	Modern and vintage buttons; artist-made buttons of clay and metal; bridal buttons and loop fasteners; buttons of pearl, rhinestone, shell, enamel, bone, horn, and more.
Chain mail websites	Chain mail, also called chain maille.
Craft stores/sites	Ribbon, chains, beads, flatback crystals, metal stampings, buttons, appliqués, trim, lace, cord, leather, faux cameos, silk/polyester flowers, studs (the craft-store name for nailheads), feathers.
Drugstores/sites	Fancy hair clips, bows, chains, bracelets, earrings, pendants, pins.
Fabric stores/sites	Appliqués, trim, ribbons, piping, cord, zippers, zipper tape, snap tape, buttons, conchos, flowers, fringe, beaded fringe, sequins, flatback crystals, fabric, Ultrasuede (the brand name for top-quality faux suede), faux fur.
Feather websites	Marabou and other boas, feather pads in amazing natural and dyed colors, loose feathers.
Fly-fishing stores/sites	Nice narrow strips of dyed rabbit fur — and the dye is waterproof.
Hardware stores/sites	Medium- to heavyweight chains, keys, keyholes, escutcheons (the little plates that go around keyholes, drawer pulls, or door handles), interesting-looking rubber washers, nuts, and hinges.
Jewelry stores/sites	Bracelets, earrings, pendants, pins, chains, charms.
Jewelry-making stores/sites	Metal stampings, beads, charms, cameos, chains, flatback crystals.
Leather-craft stores/sites	Buckles, conchos, spots (the leather-store name for nailheads), leather cord, suede fringe, bags of leather and suede scraps, snakeskin, exotic leathers, some fur.
Milliners supply stores/sites	All kinds of fabric flowers, leaves, and fruit.
Scrapbooking and rubber-stamp stores/sites	Charms, word charms, old coins, word beads, ribbons, ribbon slides, brads (the scrapbooking name for nailheads), little enamel plaques, trim, old-fashioned-looking keys, enamel tags and numbers.
Silk flower stores/sites	Silk, velvet, organdy, satin, cotton, and/or polyester flowers and leaves, ribbons.
Thrift stores/sites	Bracelets, earrings, chains, charms.
Trim stores/sites	Appliqués, trims, ribbons, piping, cord, fringe, beaded fringe, buttons, buckles, lace, flowers, nailheads (also called studs, spots, or brads), feathers, sometimes fur trim.
Home decor stores/sites	Medium- to heavyweight trim, piping, cord, braid, fringe, usually more luxurious than that found in fabric stores.
Yarn stores/sites	Buttons, especially large or of unusual designs.

Index to Techniques, Shoes, and Handbags

RESOURCES FOR YOU: OUR WEBSITE, BLOG & STORE

You'll find more ideas, how-to information, products, tools and supplies at our website, in our blog and in our online store.

The Sassy Feet **website** contains a gallery of shoes and bags, information on classes, basic how-to info, and all the articles we've had published. **www.sassyfeet.com**

Our **blog**, Glitter Sweatshop, focuses on new projects we've done — with detailed how-to instructions — and reports on our latest adventures in Shoe-It-Yourself — and Bag-It-Yourself! **http://glittersweatshop.typepad.com**

The Sassy Feet **online store** offers paints, brushes, embellishment supplies, toolkits, books and kits for doing some of our most popular designs, like Blue Haiku (Page 36) and Letters from Home (Page 39). For shipping, we charge only the amount we pay the Post Office or Fed Ex, no extra fees. **http://store.sassyfeet.com**

Last but not least, is our Sassy Feet FACEBOOK page. **http://www.facebook.com/SassyFeet**

ABOUT THE AUTHORS

Our passion is creating embellished shoes and handbags that are as meaningful as they are beautiful. Shoes carry us forward in our lives. They give us both stature and groundedness. Handbags carry our lives in miniature. Both say something about us, whether explicitly or subtly. The shoes and handbags that we create symbolize transformation, the most powerful force for good in this world. We believe there is nothing so hard or hopeless it cannot be transformed — let alone some unloved shoes or an unwisely purchased bag!

We also believe that upcycling shoes and handbags makes a statement about the harmony that can be achieved when opposites unite. Our work has artfully brought together such apparent contradictions as lace and chain maille, ribbons and Doc Martens, suede and graffiti art, the curving lines of paisley and the cage-like bars of openwork leather straps. Wouldn't the world be a wonderful place if everyone was able to find or create such *richness* in the harmony of opposites?

Margot Silk Forrest is a professional writer, writing coach and non-fiction editor. She is the author of the first edition of *Sassy Feet: How to Paint, Bead, Bedeck and Embellish Your Shoes* and *A Short Course in Kindness*. She began teaching classes on "doing" shoes in 2007 and discovered that she loved teaching this new craft as much as she loved doing it. She is a longtime member of the Peninsula Wearable Arts Guild in San Jose, CA, and lives on the central coast of California.

Destiny Carter is a freelance graphic designer and award-winning artist who works in many different media, including pencil, pen and ink, acrylics, photography, sculpture, blown glass and graphic arts. She created the logo, website and blogs designs, business cards and other graphics for Sassy Feet. Her artwork can be seen at www.destinycarter.com. She lives in Cambria, CA.

Together, Margot and Destiny run the Sassy Feet website (www.sassyfeet.com), which includes lots of shoes, bags and how-to information, an online store, and a blog full of amazing altered shoes and handbags: http://glittersweatshop.typepad.com. Their shoes have appeared in fifteen issues of *Altered Couture* magazine.

ART/WEARABLE ART EXHIBITS

- "Wearable Expressions," international juried exhibition, Palos Verdes Art Center, Palos Verdes, CA, 2008
- "Art2Wear Accoutrements: The Many Facets of Adornment" exhibition, Los Angeles Airport, 2009
- "HEARTS Obispo," ARTS Obispo Gallery, San Luis Obispo, CA, 2011
- "Walk on the Wild Side," ARTS Obispo Gallery, San Luis Obispo, CA, 2011
- "Wear Art, Thou!" Heaven and Earth Gallery, San Luis Obispo, CA, 2011
- "Shoes, Purses and Mahjong: A Few of Our Favorite Things," Janice Charach Gallery, West Bloomfield, MI, 2011

CONTACT US!

Got questions about doing shoes or bags? Got comments about the book? Write to us — we answer ALL our email!
margot@sassyfeet.com ⨍ destiny@sassyfeet.com
tel 805-771-9522 ⨍ Sassy Feet, P.O. Box 926, Morro Bay, CA 93442

46251878R00041

Made in the USA
San Bernardino, CA
01 March 2017